# Cultural Change and Biblical Faith

*The Future of the Church.*
*Biblical and Missiological Essays for the New Century*

# Cultural Change and Biblical Faith

*The Future of the Church.*
*Biblical and Missiological Essays for the New Century*

**John Drane**

paternoster
press

First Published in 2000 by Paternoster Press

06 05 04 03 02 01 00   7 6 5 4 3 2 1

Paternoster Press is an imprint of Paternoster Publishing,
P.O. Box 300, Carlisle, Cumbria, CA3 0QS, UK
Paternoster Publishing USA
P.O. Box 1047, Waynesboro, GA 30830-2047 USA
Website – www.paternoster-publishing.com

**British Library Cataloguing in Publication Data**
A catalogue record for this book is available from the British Library

ISBN 0-85364-979-0

Cover Design by Mainstream, Lancaster
Typeset by WestKey Ltd, Falmouth, Cornwall
Printed in Great Britain by Biddles Ltd,
Guildford, Surrey

# Contents

# Preface

The materials gathered together in this book were all written during the course of the last ten years of the twentieth century. The majority are appearing here in print for the first time, though a few of them have been published before in different forms. In collecting the various chapters for this book, however, they have all been revised more or less extensively, and reshaped to show how the topics with which they deal are relevant not only to understanding the cultural context in which Christians are now called to minister, but also (and more especially) to provide a focus for consideration of some crucial aspects of the nature of effective Christian witness and worship in the new situation.

Western culture is undergoing a massive paradigm shift, in the course of which our entire style of being will be radically transformed. The changes now taking place are already highlighting areas of discontinuity and contradiction that are impacting life not only in the West, but all over the world. In Western societies, I believe that we can trace two equal and opposite ways in which people are dealing with this crisis. On the one hand, many are choosing to immerse themselves in a selfish, hedonistic lifestyle that apparently has no place at all for ultimate meanings. They prefer to live only for the present, and assume that life has no meaning beyond that. At the same time, however, many others are trying to deal with the threatened disintegration of our culture by engaging in a self-conscious search for spiritual answers that will hold out the possibility of providing a secure basis on which to build new lives in the third millennium.

It is this second response to our predicament that forms the starting-point for this book. Not all of these people will be expressing their search in terminology with which Christians might instinctively feel comfortable. Some will be searching for answers by immersing themselves in social or environmental concerns, especially through involvement with single-issue pressure groups. Many more are, to a greater or lesser extent, involved with the 'alternative' spiritualities and lifestyles that have come to be associated with the New Age. Both these groups are of particular interest to Christians, because these are the people who in previous generations would have been the pillars of their local churches - yet today, they are mostly looking elsewhere for answers, because they find the church simply does not speak to their needs. Some of them may be openly hostile to the church or Christianity, though the majority have no feelings of animosity and express a quiet regret that a faith which inspired their own forebears, and in which they them-selves may have been nurtured in childhood, appears to have little to say to the changing circumstances in which their own children are growing up. These people are not against the church: they just find that what they know of it has no attraction for them. This is leading to a crisis of major proportions for the churches in the West, for our evident inability to engage with the spiritual concerns of these people is also paralleled by the growing disenchantment expressed even by some who have been lifelong church members, but who also struggle to comprehend how our present ways of being church relate to the ever-changing lifestyles and relationships in which they now find themselves. In addition – and perhaps most seriously of all – those of us who are still in the church are also mostly incapable of inspiring even our own children in ways that promote spiritual growth through adolescence and into a mature adult Christian faith.

We can no longer excuse these failures by arguing that the surrounding culture is secular and hostile to spiritual matters, for that is manifestly not the case. But when those who are looking for spiritual direction have little or no expectation of finding such a thing in the church, there are obviously some tough questions to be addressed. Asking the questions will be the easy part. Finding answers will be more difficult, not least because it is likely to demand a radical root-and-branch reformation of our ways of being church, which will inevitably involve the abandonment of some of the things we now do, as well as requiring some daring and creative thinking to reimagine what church might be like if it is to be relevant to today's culture and its lifestyles. There will be no one simple solution that can be applied everywhere, so readers should not expect to find some magic formula in the pages of this book. What I hope you will find is assistance in identifying some of the right questions as well as some signposts that may point to new directions in which we might begin to search for relevant answers.

For those who may be curious about such things, when I have quoted from the Bible I have used a variety of translations in a fairly eclectic fashion. The two standard English translations most often used are the New Revised Standard Version and the New Century Bible, though I have sometimes used my own translation, and occasionally I have combined all three.

The issues tackled here are inextricably bound up with my own spiritual pilgrimage as I have struggled to discover what it might mean for me to be Christian – especially to be a Christian theologian and minister – at this point in history. I have not sought to mask the personal dimension of the question, and I make no apologies for wearing my heart on my sleeve – for I am also a practical theologian, and the idea that we can deal adequately with any of this without also being honest about our own vulnerabilities is, for me, a denial of some central Gospel values and the exact opposite of what we now need to be in order to invite other post-modern people to join us in following Jesus.[1] Not every reader will be convinced by everything that is in here, nor would I expect them to be. But over the last decade it has all been shared in seminars and workshops with church leaders on almost every continent of the world, and I know that what I am saying has a powerful resonance with the experience of those Christians who are striving to live in ways that will honour Christ and promote the Gospel in today's post-modern environment. If it helps even one reader to engage creatively and Christianly with the culture, then the effort will be worthwhile.

I have often wondered why I have stayed in the church when so many of my generation have left it, including some of my own peers, who when I was younger often seemed to be much more religiously

---

[1] For a more nuanced articulation of this position, see Don S. Browning, *A Fundamental Practical Theology: Descriptive and Strategic Proposals* (Minneapolis: Fortress Press 1991), 7–8, who argues persuasively that, as an intellectual discipline, practical theology must begin with the experiences, situations and questions that shape the concerns of its practitioners.

committed than I ever felt. There have been times in my life when it would certainly have been easier to give up on active Christain belief. For two decades I worked in an aggressively secular university where my high-profile relationship with the Scottish churches was frequently regarded as a liability, and the system would undoubtedly have rewarded me had I toned it down or abandoned it altogether. But a significant factor in encouraging me to keep the faith during those years has undoubtedly been the opportunity to see at first hand the church in its global context. Not only has my exposure to other cultures highlighted for me the moral and spiritual bankruptcy of the West, and the inbuilt tendency of its Enlightenment-inspired educational system to identify narrow-minded bigotry with self-defined principles of 'universal reason', which can then be imposed on the rest of the world, but I have also come to realize that what we see of the church in the West is only a very small part of the total picture, and not the most exciting part by a very long way.

I owe an enormous debt of gratitude to many individuals and groups, who have not only tolerated my personal idiosyncrasies but have actively encouraged me in the kind of experimentation in applied theology that is advocated here. Among them I would particularly single out the faculty of the School of Theology at Fuller Seminary, California, who throughout the 1990s have allowed their summer courses to be used as a laboratory for these ideas by repeatedly inviting me to return along with my wife and partner Olive to teach creative subjects together in creative ways. Raymond Fung, Chinese evangelist and one-time Evangelism Secretary at the World Council of Churches, was more influential than he realized when he invited Olive and me to join him to lead an international School of Evangelism in Adelaide in 1990, for he introduced us to the world church which has been such an inspiration, and has also regularly provided a platform on which to explore the connection between Gospel and culture. I also need to include my colleagues in the University of Aberdeen, who welcomed my crazy ideas more warmly than I could ever have imagined when I joined them in 1998. Without the encouragement of all these, and the many enthusiastic participants in seminars, workshops, conferences and courses in theological colleges and seminaries all around the world, I would never have become excited about most of these topics, still less written about them.

John Drane

# Chapter 1

# The Challenge of Cultural Change[1]

'You cannot step twice into the same river, for other waters are
continually flowing on.' The words are from Heraclitus, five hundred years before the time of Christ,[2] but they could have been
written yesterday. From primeval rainforests to urban slums, today's
world is in a state of constant change. In the past cultural change was
usually a slow business, as one generation succeeded another and
made its own minor adjustments to social habits and ways of
thinking. But now change is neither subtle nor gradual: it is
traumatic and immediate. The impact of accelerating cultural
change is evident wherever we look, and no matter how fast they
run institutional leaders find it impossible to keep up with new
directions that seem to be random and unpredictable, and therefore
impossible to control or plan for.

> As the rate of change increases, the complexity of the problems that
> face us also increases. The more complex these problems are, the more
> time it takes to solve them. The more the rate of change increases, the
> more the problems that face us change and the shorter is the life of the
> solutions we find to them. Therefore, by the time we find solutions to
> many of the problems that face us, usually the most important ones, the
> problems have so changed that our solutions to them are no longer
> relevant or effective . . . As a result we are falling further and further
> behind our times.[3]

---

[1] This chapter originally appeared as 'Salvation and Cultural Change', in
*Windows on Salvation*, ed. Donald English (London: Darton, Longman & Todd,
1994), 166–180. It has been updated and supplemented here.

[2] Plato, *Cratylus* 402a.

[3] R. Ackoff, *Creating the Corporate Future* (New York: John Wiley & Sons, 1981),
4–5.

Moreover, it is not just that things are changing faster than ever before, but the actual nature of change itself seems to have changed. In the words of transpersonal psychologist Marilyn Ferguson, 'We are living in the change of change . . . the entire culture is undergoing trauma and tensions that beg for new order'.[4]

## Cultural Change

If culture is about the way people live and relate to each other,[5] then Europeans need look no further than their own continent for evidence of massive change and uncertainty. In 1984, it looked as if the world had escaped the kind of apocalyptic disintegration envisaged in George Orwell's novel of that name, and that life was set to continue in a path of linear progression into the twenty-first century. The reality has turned out to be much closer to the predictions of doom than most of us would like to admit. From the vantage point of what now seems like the security of the 1980s, few people could have imagined that by the end of the twentieth century communism would have crumbled, the map of Europe would have been significantly redrawn, and that in the process ancient tribal animosities would be resurrected in a bloodbath of ethnic cleansing, putting fear into Western powers that once again Europe might yet be plunged into savagery and chaos at the hands of fascist powers that would threaten accepted standards of behaviour and potentially undermine the stability of the continent and its culture. Up to the point of writing, Western Europe has escaped the worst horrors of the social upheaval in the East, but the collapse of the Berlin Wall did not herald the arrival of a capitalist utopia, nor has the European Union emerged as the solution to all Europe's problems. Economic and social co-operation, let alone political union, can seem little more than elusive shadows, and the inability

---

[4]  M. Ferguson, *The Aquarian Conspiracy* (London: Paladin, 1982), 30, 77.
[5]  On the nature of culture, see Bernard Waites et al., *Popular Culture: Past and Present* (London: Croom Helm, 1982); Rosamund Billington et al., *Culture and Society* (London: Macmillan, 1991). And on cultural change, Ivan Brady and Barry Isaac, *A Reader in Cultural Change* (New York: John Wiley & Sons, 1975); Jeffrey C. Alexander and Steven Seidman, *Culture and Society: Contemporary Debates* (Cambridge: CUP, 1990).

of Western leaders to address effectively the tragic events repeatedly played out on their own Eastern borders has only served to high-light the scale of the problem. In both East and West, Europe has little clear sense of either identity or purpose, and some are now asking bigger and more disturbing questions. What exactly is 'Europe'? In what sense is Europe an identifiable place? Are these countries bound together only by the fact that for centuries they shared a common history? Does the idea of 'Europe' depend more on religion and ideology than on geography and ethnicity? Was 'Europe' a notion that only made sense while the culture of Christendom provided otherwise disparate nations with a common worldview and values? Can a Europe bereft of such an ideological foundation ever hold together, or will it eventually revert to being what it physically is, just an appendage to Asia?

In a different way, the USA faces similar questions of national and cultural identity. For forty years after the end of World War II, American values and national identity were largely shaped by the perceived threat from the old Soviet Union and its allies around the world. Despite all the rhetoric about upholding traditional American values, what Ronald Reagan once dubbed the 'evil empire' was in effect calling many of the shots in US policy, domestic as well as foreign. Now the USA is forced onto the defen-sive trying to redefine its role and identity in the new world order, and it faces the same internal ambiguities as Europe. When the five-hundredth anniversary of Columbus's voyages of exploration to the 'new world' came up in 1992, Americans had no idea how to mark the occasion, let alone celebrate it, because it raised awkward questions about their cultural identity. Who are the real Americans? Certainly few would now claim that they are the Caucasian descen-dants of European explorers and immigrants, even though they are the people who still hold most of the power. In reality, today's Americans are an amalgam of many nations, with native Americans, African-Americans, Asian-Americans, Hispanic-Americans, as well as Caucasians – and others – living together in what, in cultural terms, is an uneasy truce that needs little provocation before the cracks begin to show.

There is exactly the same cultural uncertainty in other places where European travellers have settled. Even the casual visitor to Australia can sense that a great burden of corporate guilt hangs over much of the nation, as its immigrant leaders struggle to come to terms with the way their ancestors systematically destroyed the culture of Aboriginal Australians. As recently as the 1960s, state governments were sending raiding parties into Aboriginal home-lands to kidnap children to be brought up by white city dwellers and integrated into what was supposed to be a more civilized culture. It is still not uncommon to find white residents who think of them-selves as Europeans first, Australians second, and Asians not at all. European settlement of New Zealand began more auspiciously with the Treaty of Waitangi (1840) guaranteeing land rights to the original inhabitants, but that was soon discarded by white settlers who now regret it, though they are not consumed with the deep guilt of their Australian counterparts, and can at least use their country's original name of Aotearoa. Exactly the same process, with much more suffering along the way, has taken place in South Africa.

While people of European descent look within to patch up their own failing vision, the world centre of gravity is moving elsewhere. The economic power of the West has been declining ever since World War II, though the inherited wealth of the previous five hundred years made it possible for Westerners still to imagine they were truly in control of things. Today that is no longer the case. The majority of the world's people have always lived in the two-thirds world, and now they are getting influence commensurate with their numbers. The Pacific Rim is the world's economic powerhouse, and we can expect other parts of the two-thirds world increasingly to take responsibility for setting the agenda in the next century and beyond.

The influence of the developing world is not just economic, however. It has its own rich cultural heritage which the West is being forced to recognize, not least in relation to religious belief. The rise of so-called 'Islamic fundamentalism' is one of the most obvious expressions of a culture that is different from contemporary Western values, though the extent to which this is a 'threat' to the West has been overrated by the Western media, which is generally militantly anti-Muslim.[6] In even more countries Christianity is a

---

[6] On the Western press and Islam, see N. Daniel, *Islam and the West: The Making of an Image* (Edinburgh: Edinburgh University Press, 1960); E. W. Said, *Covering Islam: How the Media and the Experts Determine How We See the Rest of the World* (London: Routledge & Kegan Paul, 1985).

major force. Secular Westerners may find it hard to believe that in world terms Christianity is not declining, but growing very rapidly. As Westerners question and reject their traditional faith, the ever-increasing populations of the two-thirds world are embracing Christianity in vast numbers. In excess of 60 per cent of all the world's Christians now live in the developing world.[7] Even the Christian missionary enterprise is rapidly moving into reverse gear as Christians travel from places like Africa and South America to share their faith in the traditional Christian heartlands of Europe, North America and Australasia.[8] Alongside the shift in the world's economic centre of gravity from the West to the Pacific there is another great shift in the centre of gravity of Christian faith. For its first thousand years, Christianity was the faith of the Mediterranean lands where it originated. During its second thousand years, it was the faith of people in Europe and the lands to which they emigrated. At the beginning of its third millennium, Christianity is without question the faith of the people of the two-thirds world. That has already led to the emergence of distinctive ways of being church, as Christians have been forced to wrestle with the realities of life for those who are poor and marginalized, and have begun to ask what kind of cultural ethos will accurately reflect the message of Christ in such circumstances.[9]

## Christians and Western Culture

If Christianity is growing fast in other parts of the world, why does it apparently have so little to offer the changing culture of the West? The answer to that question is bound up with the church's role in

[7] For statistics on this, see David B. Barrett (ed.), *World Christian Encyclopedia* (New York: OUP, 1982), and regular updates published by him in a variety of journals, most accessibly the *International Bulletin of Missionary Research*.
[8] It has been calculated that by the beginning of the century, 55% of all Protestant missionaries would be non-Western. Cf. J. H. Kraakevik and D Welliver, *Partners in the Gospel* (Wheaton: Billy Graham Center, 1992), 161–175.
[9] Most notably in the rise of Liberation Theology, though by no means limited to that. Cf. T. Witvliet, *A Place in the Sun* (Maryknoll, NY: Orbis, 1985); P Berryman, *Liberation Theology* (London: Tauris, 1987); Robert McAfee Brown, *Liberation Theology: An Introductory Guide* (Louisville, KY: Westminster/John Knox Press, 1993).

the development of modern Western culture, and before we can say anything useful about the contribution that Christian faith might now make in the present context of upheaval and change, we need first to review, however briefly, what has been going on in Western thinking over the past few centuries.

Before the voyages of people like Columbus, Europeans held a simple worldview that was rooted in the dim mists of ancient history. The earth was a flat disc, and the centre of the universe. Underneath was the world of the dead, up aloft was heaven, and as long as God was in heaven, all was well. Keeping God there was a matter of doing the right things in the right places at the right times, and consequently religion permeated the whole of life. For peasant farmers, sowing seeds and other agricultural operations had religious overtones, and for politicians, national strategies were invariably bound up with religious observance.

The discovery that Europe was less than half the world was a shock to people who had known nothing else, and the success of the explorers provided a major impetus to others who threw themselves with great energy into the search for new light on other hitherto unknown aspects of human existence. When Copernicus (1473–1543) concluded that the universe must be heliocentric, not geocentric, and when the Italian astronomer Galileo (1564–1642) then popularized the idea, they found themselves on a collision course with the establishment. But the new view prevailed, a concept that had been held since the beginning of time was discarded, and there was a paradigm shift of massive dimensions that merely gave permission to others to ask further questions. New discoveries were made at breathtaking speed. Barriers began to fall in every area of human understanding. Great advances in knowledge of the physical universe became everyday occurrences. Following the lead of René Descartes (1596–1650) and Isaac Newton (1642–1727), scientists explored and articulated 'laws of nature' that would give a coherent explanation for things that previously seemed semi-miraculous – and another major paradigm shift in human understanding was under way, this time concerned with the nature of knowledge and what is worth knowing. The age of the rationalist-materialist was about to dawn. In due course there was the development of medical science, along with the Industrial Revolution, the emergence of technology and the invention of modern forms of transportation. As 'new worlds' were opened up, the developing self-confidence of the European Enlightenment was spread far beyond its own continent, and that phenomenon we now call 'Western culture' or 'modernity' came to birth: a total worldview and way of life that would ultimately – for good or ill – leave no part of the globe wholly untouched by its influence.

Alongside the scientific and technological achievements, new philosophical and religious concepts played an increasingly significant role. The discoveries that catapulted humanity from the medieval world into the modern age had not been revealed by divine intervention, but emerged progressively over time as human reason was applied to life's ultimate questions, in the search for 'scientific' answers. In that light, it seemed obvious that modern people could live quite happily without the assistance of superstition and mythology (including religion) to explain the meaning of things. In due course, the barriers of the physical world itself were broken, and a human being was sent into space. When Yuri Gagarin returned from his historic space flight in 1961, and proudly declared that he had seen no sign of God up there, that seemed to be a fitting epitaph for any kind of religious worldview. Given the time, money and expertise, nothing now seemed impossible. When scientists could give precise answers to every question, who needed God as a means of explaining things?

Looking back from the perspective of today's world, all that seems deceptively simple, if not quaint and idealistic. For even as Yuri Gagarin circled the earth with his confident message of technology come of age, storm clouds were gathering which in the ensuing thirty years would radically change the contours of much of the familiar cultural landscape. Today, the heady optimism of the past has been swept away. The old certainties of the Enlightenment are no longer secure, and there is a widespread feeling that science and technology have ultimately failed to deliver the goods. The values of modernity are being questioned at every level, both pragmatic and ideological. No one would wish to turn the clock back, of course, or deny the usefulness of the advances in human knowledge that have taken place in the course of the last two or three centuries. But more attention is now focusing on the negatives, and the foundational concepts of the whole Enlightenment vision are being subjected to radical questioning. From a scientific angle, the old Newtonian paradigm was challenged by Einstein's theory of relativity as long ago as the 1930s. But its mechanistic model for understanding everything, from people to the cosmos, still continued to dominate long after its theoretical base had been eroded. In conjunction with the thoroughgoing application of a reductionist approach to knowledge, it has created problems and discontinuities in every area of life, from the depersonalization of modern scientific medicine, to the pollution of the environment.

Perhaps more than any other single factor, it is the environmental issue that has led to the questioning and rejection of the old scientific paradigm. People had always assumed that science and technology would give us the power to determine our own destiny. Of course, it was recognized that such power might be used to both good and bad effect. But in the past it seemed possible to undo or forestall any harm that might occur. In the days of the cold war, everyone knew the potential danger of nuclear holocaust, but behind all the rhetoric there was always the unspoken assumption that, being people of common sense and rationality, the leaders of both Kremlin and White House would understand the futility of pushing the button, and would therefore desist from doing so. We were right: human reason did prevail. But the environmental crisis is not susceptible to that kind of resolution, for we have now unleashed forces that no amount of human reason will be able to control. For the first time since the Middle Ages people see their ultimate future destiny lying in the control of unknown, and probably unknowable, natural forces. Human reason enabled us to know how to make holes in the ozone layer, but it cannot tell us how to patch them up again, and as a result we still live with the frightening possibility that we may yet be fried alive in our own lifetime. Whether or not that doomsday scenario comes to pass, there is little that anyone can do about it. The great promise of Enlightenment science was that it would enable us to control our environment, rather than the environment controlling us. Now that possibility looks to be slipping away, it increasingly seems that the rationalist-materialist-reductionist outlook can no longer supply satisfactory answers to today's most urgent questions.

So what has gone wrong? Has something important been lost during the past few centuries? There is an insistence in many circles that nothing less than another radical paradigm shift will suffice, this time abandoning the mechanistic models of the past to adopt a more holistic view of things. 'In contrast to the mechanistic Cartesian view of the world, the worldview emerging from modern physics can be characterized by words like organic, holistic and ecological. The universe is no longer seen as a machine made of a multitude of objects, but has to be pictured as one indivisible, dynamic whole whose parts are essentially interrelated and can be understood only as patterns of a cosmic process.'[10] Such talk of interconnectedness at once raises questions that are of an essentially spiritual or mystical nature. Physicist Fritjof Capra has made the connection quite explicitly, claiming that the new holistic paradigm will be 'similar to the views of mystics of all ages and traditions'.[11] Instead of searching for rational explanations of everything, then, should we not be looking for 'spiritual' solutions to the crisis in our culture? Instead of trusting our logic, would it not be wiser to depend more on our intuition? Questions like that can be uncomfortable for people who have been educated to believe that human reason has the answer to everything, and the way to understand things is by taking them to pieces to analyse them. It is precisely as a result of our over-dependence on analytical thinking for so long that Western culture now has no idea where to look for spiritual or emotional direction.

The problem is exacerbated by the fact that the traditional Western source of spiritual guidance – the church – is perceived as a part of the old cultural establishment that seems to have created our present predicament.[12] It is debatable whether Christian values shaped the Enlightenment, or whether the church allowed itself to be taken over by essentially secular values, but either way the practical outcome is the same: if Christianity is part of the problem it cannot also be part of the solution. Management professor Russell

---

[10]  Paul Davies, *Society and the Rising Culture* (London: Flamingo, 1989), 66.

[11]  F. Capra, *The Turning Point* (London: Flamingo, 1983), xvii.

[12]  On this, see Capra, *Turning Point*, especially 21–22 where he lists the characteristics of the 'old age' in terms that are too close for comfort to traditional Christian attitudes: 'masculine, demanding, aggressive, competitive, rational, analytic . . .' For a remarkably similar analysis (though from a Christian perspective, and therefore reaching different conclusions), see Lesslie Newbigin, *Foolishness to the Greeks* (Geneva: WCC, 1986); *The Gospel in a Pluralist Society* (London: SPCK, 1989).

Ackoff has openly stated that we will not successfully make the transition from what he calls the Machine Age to the Systems Age unless we jettison Christian belief.[13]

Consequently, the only place to look for spiritual guidance will either be other cultures and worldviews, or within ourselves – and both of these are playing a significant part in the rising culture. For some, it leads to the adoption of Asian spirituality, especially Buddhism, or even Islam.[14] For others, it involves rediscovering and accepting native cultures that were displaced by European invasions of the Americas, Australasia or Africa, all of whose people seem to have been able to live at peace with themselves and their environment in a way that we are unable to do. This particular route to a new worldview also has the advantage of facilitating the expiation of some of the West's corporate guilt about its past treatment of these cultures. Yet others find a solution in what is effectively a reversal of history, by jumping backwards over the Christian period into the pagan past of Europe itself, to embrace and affirm the long-lost values and worldviews of our own ancestors. Others again seek solace in transpersonal psychology, encouraged by the apparent similarity between its techniques and the experience of mystics through the ages.[15] As a result, a dazzling and bewildering array of different spiritualities compete for attention, each of them claiming to offer something that will help us find our souls again, and chart a safe course into the new culture of the future. The goods on offer in this religious marketplace range from messages from spirit guides and extraterrestrials to neo-paganism, Celtic mythology and aboriginal spirituality – not to mention renewed interest in astrology and a vast range of psychological therapies, all holding out the prospect of a renewed, holistic humanity.

---

[13] Ackoff, *Creating the Corporate Future*, 19–20.

[14] Increasing numbers of Western people are converting to Islam, mostly as Western women marry into Muslim families, but also significant numbers of Afro-Caribbeans who find themselves alienated by Western cultural values, and others who are attracted by the strenuous moral demands Islam places on believers.

[15] On the connection between transpersonal psychology and the emerging spirituality, see R. S. Valle, 'The Emergence of Transpersonal Psychology', in R. S. Valle and S. Halling (eds), *Existential-Phenomenological Perspectives in Psychology* (New York: Plenum Press, 1989), 257–268.

Inevitably, the post-modern[16] culture that is now rising in the West is quite different from what preceded it. At one and the same time, it combines an acceptance of many of the fruits of science and technology with a questioning of the worldview that produced them, and what looks like a return to something similar to the ancient spirituality of the pre-critical age. It therefore poses a far-reaching challenge to many accepted cultural norms, not least the notion of objective truth and the role of reason in establishing truth. Bhagwan Shree Rajneesh summed it up neatly with the claim that 'It is not that the intellect sometimes errs; it is that the intellect is the error'.[17] That is a massive challenge to Western life as we have known it. On the one hand, it can manifest itself in the actions of someone like Charles Manson, who could butcher a house full of people and insist that nothing had really happened because on a holistic worldview 'all is one', and so there is no such thing as good or evil.[18] On the other, it might emerge as a revisionist account of Nazi history, in which the holocaust never took place – or, for that matter, in a rewriting of the history of ancient Celtic Christianity to make it more amenable to contemporary New Age spirituality.

The observer who simply wants to know what is going on will not find it easy to understand all this, not least because the cultural and intellectual goalposts are being moved all the time. In spiritual terms, this is all easily lumped together as 'the New Age Movement' – but that description itself is a misnomer, because it makes it sound like the work of a minority pressure group. Whatever is happening is certainly much bigger than that, and is here to stay. Though none of this is a 'movement' in the sense of belonging to some organization – still less being part of a conspiracy – the term 'movement' does accurately capture the fluid and dynamic feel of things, which in turn explains why some people refuse to take it seriously as a real cultural change. Ernest Gellner has articulated the feelings of many with his wry comment that 'Postmodernism is a contemporary movement. It is strong and fashionable. Over and above this, it is

---

[16] For the distinction between 'post-modern' and 'postmodern' see my explanation on p. 94–5.

[17] Bhagwan Shree Rajneesh, *I am the Gate* (New York: Harper & Row, 1977), 18.

[18] Cf. R. C. Zaehner, *Our Savage God* (New York: Sheed & Ward, 1974).

not altogether clear what the devil it is. In fact, clarity is not conspic-
uous amongst its marked attributes' – though he does not miss the
key fact that 'the notion of objective reality is suspect – all this seems
to be part of the atmosphere, or mist, in which postmodernism
flourishes, or which postmodernism helps to spread'.[19]

## The Gospel and the Rising Culture

What does the gospel have to say in this context? Asking questions is
the easy part. Answering them will be a challenging, even painful
business for the Christian church. We cannot ignore the repeated
claim that the Western Christian tradition as we know it is part of
the problem, and is therefore unlikely to be part of the solution.
Some of the negative things being said about Christianity are
certainly either untrue or exaggerated. But there is more than just a
hint of truth in most of them, and repentance will be a more appropriate response than self-justification, especially in relation to such
matters as the pollution of the environment under the influence of
the Calvinist work ethic, the exploitation of women, children and
native populations around the world, and the perpetuation of unjust
and often racist systems of government. Before Christians can bring
good news to the lives of others, they will need to rediscover for
themselves the renewing power of God's Spirit: 'the call to conversion should begin with the repentance of those who do the
calling'.[20] This applies not only to Christian attitudes to socio-
political issues, but also to matters that may seem related to the heart
of faith itself and its spirituality. For here too, many serious spiritual
searchers regard the ways we now worship and witness as part of
the problem, which means that doing more of the same will
resolve nothing.[21]

---

[19] Ernest Gellner, *Postmodernism, Reason and Religion* (London: Routledge,
1992), 22, 23. On the New Age more generally, see my *What Is the New Age Still
Saying to the Church?* (London: HarperCollins, 1999).
[20] *Mission and Evangelism: An Ecumenical Affirmation* (Geneva: WCC, 1982),
section 13.
[21] On this, and much of what follows, see my *Faith in a Changing Culture*
(London: HarperCollins, 1997).

'The medium is the message', and the way Christians have communicated their message has often betrayed the good news they claim to have. There have been dissenting voices in every generation, but from the time of Constantine's conversion onwards the Western church has generally allowed itself to be used as a channel for secular culture, rather than critiquing prevailing assumptions by reference to gospel values.[22] When imperialist expansion was high on the Western cultural agenda, whether at the time of the Crusades, or the conquest of South America, or the nineteenth-century missionary movement, our forebears needed an imperialistic God, and the church was not slow to supply the need. All too often, 'salvation' was taken to the ends of the earth at the sharp end of a sword. Even today, when that is no longer literally possible, our evangelistic efforts often have a macho image reminiscent of Hollywood movies at their worst. Arrogance has its own reward, and by being pliable the church can become enormously rich and influential, as it was during the period of Christendom. But that itself only highlights the intrinsic discontinuity between where we find ourselves and what we say we believe. For at the heart of the gospel is not an image that shows God as an all-conquering monarch, but a different emphasis on a God who became a child. The first disciples felt uncomfortable about that, and it has caused problems for power-hungry church leaders ever since. The Christian message is not about transcendence and power, but about weakness, vulnerability, and powerlessness.

Taking the implications of that seriously will make a significant difference to many aspects of Christian witness in today's world. It relates to the kind of language we use about God, the structures we tolerate in our churches, the way women, men and children of

---

[22] The various possible models for the interaction of Christian faith and culture have been well explored in such classic works as H. Richard Niebuhr, *Christ and Culture* (New York: Harper & Row, 1951), or Charles H. Kraft, *Christianity in Culture* (Maryknoll, NY: Orbis, 1979); and in more pragmatic terms in works such as Bruce J. Nicholls, *Contextualization: A Theology of Gospel and Culture* (Exeter: Paternoster Press, 1979), and J. R. W. Stott and R. Coote, *Down to Earth: Studies in Christianity and Culture* (London: Hodder & Stoughton, 1981). But overall it is still much easier to find examples of Christianity allowing itself to be taken over by the prevailing culture, than challenging and questioning it.

different life experiences find acceptance and affirmation among us, not to mention our styles of worship, the ways we teach and expect people to learn – and even the designs we adopt for church buildings. Being faithful to the gospel vision will also bring us into conflict with certain aspects of post-modern culture, notably its tendency to underplay the reality of evil. For alongside the 'pick-and-mix' approach to spirituality, our culture also has a supermarket mentality about lifestyles, in which people choose to be who they are. In the words of one spiritual commentator, 'We create the realities we experience . . . The universe ultimately gives us what we ask for . . . Since we construct our own lives it is false and misleading to blame others for what we are experiencing . . .'[23] That can sound like good news to middle-class Western yuppies but it is decidedly bad news to the poor and the oppressed, in our own society as well as the rest of the world – and it is completely at odds with the teaching of Jesus, who on encountering those who were sinned-against did not blame them for their predicament, but had compassion on them.

What is the Christian answer? We will certainly need to insist on the objective reality of evil and suffering in the world (no doubt as part of a wider insistence on the existence of objective reality in general). But we should also ask what sin really is. It is easy for Christians who are comfortable to define sin as something that other people do, and of which they therefore need to repent. That has often been the starting point for evangelization.[24] But a message that starts by putting people down will never be good news. Nor is it the message of Jesus, who always lifted up those who were wounded and broken, and whose primary call was to 'Follow me.' It was in the process of following that disciples discovered the enormity of sin – and their part in it – and realized the need for personal repentance and radical change. In biblical terms, sin is about a breakdown of relationships, not only between people, but between people and the natural environment, as well

[23] J. L. Simmons, *The Emerging New Age* (Santa Fe: Bear & Co., 1990), 83.
[24] It was also the theological foundation on which Thatcherism was built in the 1980s: cf. M. Novak, *The Spirit of Democratic Capitalism* (New York: Simon & Schuster, 1982); D. Anderson (ed.), *The Kindness that Kills* (London: SPCK, 1984); J. Davies (ed.), *God and the Marketplace* (London: Institute of Economic Affairs, Health and Welfare Unit, 1993).

as people and God.[25] To view sin in exclusively personal terms is theologically shallow and inevitably leads to a deviant view of salvation, with the accompanying conclusion that the gospel is a commodity to be marketed, rather than an all-embracing truth that challenges the whole of life.

There are also important questions relating to the part the church might play in becoming a channel of salvation for our culture. One of the major contemporary trends is the emergence of so-called 'designer lifestyles', as people seek identity and satisfaction not from employment, but from leisure. In the future there will be fewer and fewer full-time jobs, and whether by necessity or choice people will need to take responsibility for designing their own lifestyle package. People will increasingly do things because they want to do them, and they believe in them, not because they are expected to do them. Coupled with early retirement and unemployment, that will mean more and more people looking around for causes to which to commit themselves.[26] Businesses are already well aware of the need to maximize the support of everyone who relates to their products, including suppliers and consumers as well as their own employees, and have created structures capable of receiving feedback and input from these so-called 'stakeholders'.[27] Churches, however, tend to be closed organizations. Some present so many hurdles to be negotiated before acceptance is achieved that it is a wonder anyone at all ever makes it. Many will find themselves attracted to what Christianity seems to be about, but how easy will it be for the church to accept them?

We also need to tackle the related assumption that God only works in the church. The biblical view is that God is at work in the world all the time, and always has been. To believe otherwise is to have a very strange – and certainly unchristian – view of God. Theories about salvation only translate into experiences of salvation when Christians recognize what God is doing out there, get alongside God and other people, and in the process 'give an account of the hope that is within them' (1 Peter 3:15). That involves

---

[25] This theme is further developed in Chapter 4 below, particularly in relation to the work of influential ex-Dominican theologian Matthew Fox.

[26] Cf. Charles Handy, *The Age of Unreason* (London: Business Books, 1989), 137–402.

[27] Cf. R. Ackoff, *Creating the Corporate Future*, 25–49; Charles Handy, *Understanding Organizations* (London: Penguin, 4th edn, 1993), *passim*.

listening to others, as well as speaking with them. It means resisting the temptation to think of ourselves as packagers and marketers of a religious product which people may take if they want (they typically don't). It means taking the incarnation seriously, and ourselves becoming childlike in order to enter the Kingdom. It means building bridges towards other people who are not yet believers, facing the challenge of Jesus' question, 'Who are my friends?' (Matthew 12:46–50). It means putting people before programmes. On a personal level (and most threateningly of all, perhaps), it means recognizing that we have something to share with other people not because we are different from them, but precisely because we are no different. Their concerns are ours, and we stand in solidarity with them because of our humanity. But we try to see things the way God sees them, and that is what makes a difference.[28]

Finally – and perhaps most challenging of all – the church faces some hard questions about its attitude to the supernatural, the mystical, and the numinous. Our evident embarrassment in this area is one of the legacies from the old rationalist-materialist paradigm. But with the rising tide of hands-on spiritual experience in our culture, a non-supernatural version of the gospel is unlikely to serve us well, and if we persist with it we will only succeed in marginalizing Christian faith even further. The work of Matthew Fox will come in for some strident criticism in later chapters of this book, but on this theme he continually puts his finger on the crucial issues that Christians now need to deal with. He makes a telling point when he connects the absence of the mystical from our religious institutions with some of the major social ailments of Western culture: 'Drugs, I believe, are inevitable if a culture fails to offer means of transcendence to the young.' We need to affirm the importance of reason as a God-given faculty, while also acknowledging that there is a non-rational dimension to human fulfilment that is not the same as the irrationality for which so many seem to be opting. In the process, the church's worship will need to be revitalized and renewed, for (as Fox goes on to observe), 'worship is the normal route for providing such experiences of transcendence' – though later in the same book he asks why worship so rarely seems to

---

[28] For more on this, Cf. Raymond Fung, 'Mission in Christ's Way', in *International Review of Mission* 79 (1990), 4–29; *The Isaiah Vision* (Geneva: WCC, 1992).

deliver its promises, and suggests that it is because we are 'saddled with forms from the modern era that prevent prayer from happening.'[29] He is right, and for worship to be reinstated as a radical, mystical experience of God in Christ that also points in Biblical fashion well beyond the interior experience of the individual and out to the world, indeed the whole cosmos, will require a radical transformation of much of what now passes as church. This is unlikely to be an easy or painless transformation, because most of us are out of our depth when dealing with such possibilities. But if the obvious alternative is for the church to continue to decline and, perhaps sooner than we imagine, die altogether in the West, then those who are committed to following Christ and to discerning God's will for this generation cannot and must not shirk the challenge just because it happens to be personally threatening and ecclesiastically disruptive.

In contemplating this challenge, one of the most encouraging verses in the Bible is Matthew 28:17. Its significance is usually overshadowed by what follows, the 'Great Commission', a passage that over the centuries has had more than its fair share of imperialistic misrepresentation. In reality, what precedes it undermines that kind of interpretation, for Matthew records that 'When [the disciples] saw [Jesus] they worshipped him, even though some of them doubted'. Faced with the challenge of taking the gospel to their own culture, the disciples' starting point was their own weakness. They were people with at least as much doubt as faith, who were prepared to take their message onto other people's territory not in order to conquer it, but with an overwhelming sense of their own inadequacy and vulnerability. No one can read the New Testament and fail to be inspired by their achievement: they were the most successful generation of Christian evangelists there has ever been. But they knew what we easily forget: that with God, ordinary people can accomplish extraordinary things. The church is growing in the two-thirds world today largely through the apparently unspectacular witness of ordinary Christians, often children and women. If we could bring ourselves to learn from them, that would be really good news, not only for the church but also for the wider culture which is desperately searching for new direction, and in which we are called to bear witness to our faith.

---

[29] Matthew Fox, *Confessions* (San Francisco: HarperSanFrancisco, 1996), 11, 251.

# Chapter 2

# Methods and Perspectives in Understanding the New Age[1]

Reference has already been made to the New Age. But what exactly is it? Like many other questions, the answer we might give to that one depends to a considerable extent on the vantage point from which we are observing the contemporary spiritual search of our culture. In the early 1990s, British tabloid newspapers created an image of New Agers as gangs of unkempt, drug-crazed travellers living in old buses parked illegally on other people's property, in the vicinity of places like Stonehenge and other ancient 'spiritual' sites. In the USA, on the other hand, the New Age will forever be linked with Hollywood actress Shirley Maclaine and her TV mini-series, *Out on a Limb*, portraying the New Age not as a concern of social drop-outs, but as the playground of the rich and famous, searching for a spiritual dimension to life because they already had everything else.[2] Members of the British royal family have also been known to connect with this kind of spiritual search – and there is not a major city anywhere in the world which does not host a regular exhibition related to 'mind, body, and spirit'. Here, the makers of witch's broomsticks typically rub shoulders with the saffron-robed devotees of ISKCON, while crystal healers stand alongside students of ancient Coptic Gnostic texts, tarot card readers, specialists in past-life recall, Kirlian photographers, channellers of spirit guides, aficionados in extraterrestrial intelligence, and therapists of every conceivable variety – to mention

---

[1] This chapter is a revised version of an article previously published under the same title in *Themelios* 23/2 (1998), 22–34.

[2] The mini-series was based on Maclaine's autobiography of the same title: *Out on a Limb* (London: Bantam), 1983).

only a tiny sample of what might be on offer. Nor are these things confined to large urban centres, for most small communities boast their psychic fairs, while one of the surprising growth industries of the last two decades has been the unprecedented spread of metaphysical bookstores.

## Definitions

It is easy enough to describe and document all this activity. But what makes these things 'new age'? In her history of the Findhorn Foundation, Carol Riddell describes life there as 'a spiritual super-market, with all kinds of different "products" on the shelves to sample'.[3] She provides a bewildering list of what might be included in these products: Buddhism, Hatha Yoga, Ta'i Chi, Sufism, Transcen-dental Meditation, organic food, past-life therapy, *A Course in Miracles*, as well as various elements from the Christian tradition. She goes on to indicate that 'all this makes up what has been described as the "new age" movement'.[4] What she describes is a mere drop in the ocean compared with what is more widely on offer. Indeed, the sheer diversity of all this led one writer to conclude that the New Age is 'a cluster of related ideas, teachings and groups, not altogether coherent, most of which would identify with this title'.[5]

Such a description is so vague as to be almost worthless, which is why others question whether the New Age really is an identifiable entity at all. Just to add even more complexity for those who like neat logical analysis, some who once happily used the term would prefer to discard it. Carol Riddell again is typical, and avers that 'We are now a little wary of this description, which was once eagerly embraced by the Findhorn Community, because in popular thought it has become connected with the sensation seekers . . . whose interest lies less in

---

[3] Carol Riddell, *The Findhorn Community: Creating a Human Destiny for the 21st Century* (Findhorn: Findhorn Press, 1990), 222. Findhorn is on the Moray Firth in north-east Scotland, and has arguably been one of the most influential New Age centres anywhere in the world.

[4] Riddell, *Findhorn Community*, 63.

[5] Denise Cush, 'British Buddhism and the New Age', in *Journal of Contemporary Religion* 11/2 (1996), 196.

seeking spiritual transformation than in dabbling in the occult, or in practising classical capitalist entrepreneurship on the naïve.'[6]

Others wish to differentiate what they regard as the 'serious' New Age search, which is concerned to uncover and articulate a new paradigm of reality, from the populist or 'glamour' New Age, which focuses more on things like the channelling of spirit guides, crystal healing, and similar phenomena.[7] There is no less diversity of opinion among serious scholars. Some regard the New Age as the outcome of Eastern religions being adapted into Western culture,[8] while others trace it back to the counter-culture of the 1960s, now transposed into a different key as that generation has reached mid-life – while for yet others it can be seen as part of a revivalist movement within the traditional Western esoteric circles inspired by people like Emanuel Swedenborg (1688–1722), Henry David Thoreau (1817–62), Ralph Waldo Emerson (1803–82), and other early American Transcendentalists, or Helena Petrovna Blavatsky (1831–91), founder of the Theosophical Society.[9]

All these understandings contain elements of truth, but no single one of them by itself can explain the amazing rise to prominence of the New Age – and it is in any case far more eclectic and more all-embracing than any or all of its apparent forerunners. Part of the difficulty of definition is related to the analytical categories within which Western scholarship has traditionally operated. We do not find it easy to imagine how anything so apparently diffuse and disorganized could also be so successful. But the truth is that there is no central organization behind the New Age, there is nothing to join, and no one way of actually being a New Ager. The movement has been variously described as a 'metanetwork', or a network of networks,[10] or a segmented polycentric integrated network

---

[6] Riddell, *Findhorn Community*, 64.

[7] Cf. David Spangler, *The Rebirth of the Sacred* (London: Gateway, 1984), 79.

[8] Cf. Colin Campbell, 'The Easternisation of the West', in Bryan Wilson and Jamie Cresswell (eds), *New Religious Movements: Challenge and Response* (London: Routledge, 1999).

[9] 'New Thought and the New Age', in J. R. Lewis and J. G. Melton (eds), *Perppectives on the New Age* (Albany, NY: State University of New York Press, 1992), 15–29.

[10] Elliot Miller, *A Crash Course on the New Age Movement* (Grand Rapids: Baker, 1989), 14.

(SPIN),[11] while from a philosophical point of view Wittgenstein's notion of 'family resemblance' can also be invoked as a possible model for understanding it.[12] Moreover, as we observed in the last chapter, the New Age is also very definitely a 'movement', in the quite literal sense that it is always on the move. Things are constantly changing, as spiritual searchers keep looking in new places, which means that almost any definition we might produce can, with perfectly good reason, be challenged by others whose experience of the phenomenon has been different. Diversity is one of the key identifying factors of today's spiritual search, and for that reason alone the effort to identify a single theological perspective that will be shared by all New Agers is, by definition, doomed to ultimate failure.

## Cultural Change

In reality, the various threads that go to make up the New Age tapestry are held together not by a common ideology, but by a shared perception of the nature of contemporary cultural change. In essence, the New Age is a form of post-modernity, and as such it is part of the questioning and redefining of the values and methods inherited from the European Enlightenment, which has swept through all areas of intellectual reflection and popular culture in the last twenty years or so.[13] The New Age's answer to

---

[11] After the pioneering work of anthropologists Luther Gerlach and Virginia Hine: cf. Hine's 'The Basic Paradigm of a Future Socio-Cultural System', in *World Issues* (April/May 1977). On the New Age connection, see Marilyn Ferguson, *The Aquarian Conspiracy* (London: Paladin, 1982), 231–241; Michael York, *The Emerging Network* (Lanham, MD: Rowman & Littlefield, 1995), 324–334; Michael York, 'The New Age in Britain Today', in *Religion Today* 9/3 (1994), 14–21.

[12] L. Wittgenstein, *Philosophical Reflections* (Oxford: Blackwell, 1968), sections 65–78.

[13] The literature on modernity and postmodernism is enormous. For general orientation see Hans Bertens, *The Idea of the Postmodern* (London: Routledge, 1995); David Harvey, *The Condition of Postmodernity* (Oxford: Blackwell, 1989); Keith Tester, *The Life and Times of Post-Modernity* (London: Routledge, 1993). For Christian perspectives, see Philip Sampson et al., *Faith and Modernity* (Oxford: Regnum, 1994); Stanley J. Grenz, *A Primer on Postmodernism* (Grand Rapids:

the dislocation and collapse now apparently facing the world is that the only way forward will be through a massive transformational shift in consciousness, of cosmic proportions. As with many critiques of modernity (including Christian ones), the New Age is itself a product of this same worldview with which it expresses dissatisfaction, though unlike other critiques it also unashamedly incorporates into its solutions key elements of what can only be described as a 'pre-modern' worldview, based on a pre-scientific, essentially mythological epistemology.[14]

We have already explored in our first chapter some aspects of the cultural changes that are now taking place. A more specifically New Age understanding of all that might typically be something along the following lines:

> Our present predicament can be traced mostly to mistakes made by Western thinkers in the course of the last five hundred years, which in turn was rooted in the West's love affair with the rationality of the Greeks. This philosophy has led to the marginalization of human and spiritual values, and an unhealthy preoccupation with a mechanistic, rationalist, reductionist worldview. In the process, there has been a profound loss of spiritual perception, and if the present crisis is to be resolved that trend will have to be reversed. The recovery of spirituality must now be a top priority. Traditional Western sources of spiritual guidance will, however, be of little help in this enterprise, for the Christian church is inextricably bound up with the old cultural establishment – so much so that the defective Enlightenment worldview was, in effect, little more than the logical outcome of classical Christian beliefs and values.[15]

---

(continued) Eerdmans, 1996); David S. Dockery (ed.), *The Challenge of Postmodernism* (Wheaton, IL: Bridgepoint, 1995); Walter Truett Anderson, *Reality Isn't What it Used to Be* (San Francisco: Harper & Row, 1990); Millard J. Erickson, *Postmodernizing the Faith* (Grand Rapids: Baker, 1998).

[14] Cf. Paul Heelas, 'The New Age in Cultural Context: The Pre-Modern, the Modern and the Post-Modern', in *Religion* 23/2 (1993), 103–116.

[15] Influential examples of this kind of analysis would be the study by Marilyn Ferguson already mentioned (*The Aquarian Conspiracy*), or Fritjof Capra, *The Turning Point* (New York: Simon & Schuster, 1982). For a history of Western thinking which arrives at broadly similar conclusions, cf. Richard Tarnas, *The Passion of the Western Mind* (New York: Ballantine, 1991).

The relationship between Christianity, Enlightenment, and Western culture is not quite that simple, of course.[16] But in the New Age, as in post-modernity more generally, image and perception is everything, and once something is believed by a sufficient number of people, it becomes irrelevant whether or not it is historically accurate or literally true. For better or worse, therefore, Christianity (at least in its classical Western form) is increasingly perceived as part of the problem, and for that reason it cannot also be part of the solution: if spirituality is to be restored to today's world, it will have to come from somewhere else.

## New Age Reference Points

It is pointless to try to construct a detailed route map that will guide us through all the intricacies of New Age spirituality. The New Age can hold together beliefs and practices that, on conventional definitions of rationality, would be regarded as incompatible, logically contradictory and mutually self-exclusive. Nevertheless, it is perfectly feasible to identify some fundamental compass points that can provide a general sense of direction through the New Age maze, without being prescriptive about the actual path that any given New Ager might actually follow. My proposal has already been mentioned briefly in the last chapter, and now needs to be set out in more detail. This is not the only way to categorize the New Age spiritual quest, but it seems to me that from a theological standpoint it is possible to identify four dominant polarities through which transformational philosophies and experiences are presently being pursued within the New Age.[17]

---

[16]  Though there is more than a grain of truth in the New Age analysis. Cf. the comment of David Bebbington: 'It is extremely hard to resist the conclusion that the early evangelicals were immersed in the Enlightenment. They were participating fully in the progressive thought of their age . . .' ('The Enlightenment and Evangelicalism', in M. Eden and D. F. Wells [eds], *The Gospel in the Modern World* [Leicester: IVP, 1991], 76).

[17]  See my 'Christian Theology, New Agers and the Spiritual Search of Western Culture', in *Rutherford Journal of Church and Ministry* 1/1 (1994), 20–25; 'Christians, New Agers, and Changing Cultural Paradigms', in *Expository Times* 106/6 (1994–95), 172–176 – reprinted in *Mission Focus Annual Review* 4 (1996), 13–21; *What is the New Age Still Saying to the Church* (London: HarperCollins, 1999).

### Non-Western worldviews

That is, the traditional worldviews of Eastern religions. An attractive, if superficial, view states that, if the cause of our present predicament is rooted in things that are modern and Western, then the way to resolve it will be to seek solutions in things that are ancient and Eastern (or at least, not part of mainstream 'Western' culture). On this basis, many Western people are committing themselves to Eastern spiritual paths, particularly – but not exclusively – Buddhism, albeit in a Westernized form. A leading New Age activist, the Hollywood actress Shirley Maclaine, expressed a popular opinion when she wrote that 'this New Age is the time when the intuitive beliefs of the East and the scientific thinking of the West could meet and join – the twain wed at last'.[18]

### First-nation beliefs

Long before white Westerners settled in the Americas, or Australasia, these lands – and others like them – were home to ancient nations. The environmentally friendly lifestyles of these people were brutally suppressed, and their spirituality was devalued by Western imperialists who labelled it 'primitive' and 'unscientific'. But with the benefit of hindsight, it seems that Western people could have learned much from the traditional worldviews of aboriginal peoples. Could it therefore be that by reaffirming these values that were previously discarded, the world's peoples together might find new ways to take us forward into the future? In the process, white Westerners might also expiate some of the guilt they now feel for the behaviour of their forebears. This has become a major concern within the New Age.

### Creation-centred

Long before the spread of what we now identify as classical 'Western' values, articulated through the categories of Greek philosophy

---

[18] Shirley Maclaine, *Going Within* (London: Bantam, 1990), 99; a view put forward with some vigour (and scientific insight) by Capra, *Turning Point*; Fritjof Capra, *The Web of Life* (London: HarperCollins, 1996); see also Lawrence Krauss, *The Physics of Star Trek* (London: HarperCollins, 1996).

and spread by the might of Christendom, Europe itself was home to a different, arguably more 'spiritual' worldview. Should Western people not therefore be looking for answers within their own heritage, by the rediscovery and appropriation of the kind of worldview that inspired and motivated their own distant ancestors? This concern accounts for the burgeoning interest in neo-paganism in its many forms, which is one of the fastest-growing aspects of New Age spirituality in northern Europe today.[19]

### Person-centred

Many of those who today are searching for new ways of being have no interest at all in anything that could be called 'religion'. The development of psychotherapies of various kinds – not least the rise of transpersonal psychology – is providing this kind of ostensibly 'secular' person with access to the same kind of transformational experiences as mystical religious traditions offer, without the initially unwelcome baggage of religious dogma.[20] This explains the popularity of transformational video and audio tapes, 'bodywork' and other therapies – often supported by claims that modern physics and mathematics are 'proving' the value of all this in some kind of scientific sense.

---

[19] For an informed account of neo-paganism, see Graham Harvey, *Listening People, Speaking Earth: Contemporary Paganism* (London: Hurst & Co., 1997). There is a good deal of debate as to whether this really is a rediscovery of the past, or whether it is not an imposition on the past of a modern agenda. See, for example, discussions of the allegation that Christianity (= 'patriarchy') displaced an original goddess-centred matriarchal culture: Mary Jo Weaver, 'Who Is the Goddess and Where Does She Get Us?', in *Journal of Feminist Studies in Religion* 5/1 (1989), 49–64; Sally Binford, 'Are Goddesses and Matriarchies Merely Figments of Feminist Imagination?' in Charlene Spretnak (ed.), *The Politics of Women's Spirituality* (Garden City, NY: Doubleday, 1982), 541–549; Ronald Hutton, *The Pagan Religions of the Ancient British Isles: Their Nature and Legacy* (Oxford: Blackwell, 1991).

[20] Though there is in reality a great deal of religious baggage associated with transpersonal psychology: cf. R. S. Valle, 'The Emergence of Transpersonal Psychology', in R. S. Valle and S. Halling (eds), *Existential-Phenomenological Perspectives in Psychology* (New York: Plenum Press, 1989), 257–268.

The unique forms of New Age spirituality emerge from the interweaving of these different and ostensibly unrelated threads. But while diversity is a key empirical hallmark of the New Age, not all New Agers are equally supportive of the attempt to construct an eclectic worldview from such widely assorted materials. Some, such as David Spangler and William Irwin Thomson, are strongly in favour of the self-conscious merging of different traditions, seeing this as the only hope for our world, and in their book *Reimagination of the World* they share this vision with considerable enthusiasm, claiming among other things that

> this new planetary sensibility or culture will be less a thing and more a process that nourishes our creativity and wholeness and provides sustenance for building the bodies of tomorrow . . . we are reimagining our world. We are taking hunks of ecology and slices of science, pieces of politics and a sprinkle of economics, a pinch of religion and a dash of philosophy, and we are reimagining these and a host of other ingredients into something new: a New Age, a reimagination of the world.[21]

Others find this approach much less attractive, and in her book *The Spiral Dance*, the Wiccan writer Starhawk in effect dismisses all this as just another twist in the imperialistic stranglehold of the West over other cultures. She writes disdainfully of people who are 'spiritually starved in their own culture' and 'unwittingly become spiritual strip miners damaging other cultures in superficial attempts to uncover their mystical treasures'.[22] Carol Riddell sounds a similar warning: 'It is as if we were in a market place with many stalls offering goods. Some people go to one stall to buy, others go to another. We support each other constantly, *but the path of inner transformation is ultimately a personal one. However much we may share with others, each of us has a unique path to the Self.*'[23]

---

[21]  David Spangler and William Irwin Thomson, *Reimagination of the World* (Santa Fe: Bear & Co., 1991), xvi.

[22]  Starhawk, *The Spiral Dance* (San Francisco: Harper & Row, 1989), 214.

[23]  Riddel, *Findhorn Community*, 63, italics mine.

## Wider Connections

It is not necessary here to consider every possible connection there may be between aspects of New Age thinking and the wider world of spirituality. Rather, I wish to single out two examples to illustrate how the New Age deals with those spiritual traditions it embraces, and then to make some comments about issues of power and the wider sociological significance of the New Age in the face of contemporary cultural collapse and change.

Observers with a sense of Christian history will instinctively think of Gnosticism when they encounter the New Age. As part of this wider spiritual renaissance, there is indeed a revival of Gnostic ideas today, and even the emergence of self-consciously Gnostic 'churches' – something that we will explore in more detail in the next chapter. Carl Gustav Jung, whose insights are highly valued in many New Age circles, himself owed a debt to his study of ancient Gnosticism,[24] and one of the leading New Age journals is called simply *Gnosis*. Observing all this, Ted Peters has described the New Age as 'perennial gnosticism', because 'The new age is reminiscent of gnosticism in the ancient Roman Empire both in what it teaches and in its competitive position *vis-à-vis* Christian orthodoxy.'[25]

There are indeed some sections of the New Age which adopt what is in effect a Gnostic worldview. Sir George Trevelyan, often thought of as the 'father' of the British New Age, makes this connection explicit and traces his own spiritual lineage back to ancient Gnosticism, as mediated through the Knights Templar, the Cathars and Albigenses, Rosicrucianism and Freemasonry. Moreover, he invokes the familiar Gnostic notion of spiritual hierarchies, and sees no hope for humankind apart from a final escape from material existence into the world of spirit.[26] Those New Agers who specialize in channelling messages from spirit guides and extraterrestrials, and speculating about the lost continents of Lemuria and

---

[24] C. G. Jung, *Modern Man in Search of a Soul* (London: Paul, Trench, Trubner, 1933). Cf. June Singer, *Seeing Through the Visible World: Jung, Gnosis and Chaos* (San Francisco: Harper & Row, 1990); R. A. Segal, *The Gnostic Jung* (Princeton, NJ: Princeton University Press, 1992).

[25] Ted Peters, *The Cosmic Self* (San Francisco: HarperSanFrancisco, 1991), 55, 56.

[26] George Trevelyan, *Operation Redemption: A Vision of Hope in an Age of Turmoil* (Walpole, NH: Stillpoint Publishing, 1985).

Atlantis or legends of Arthurian Britain, also generally share this highly dualistic outlook, in which salvation can only be found through the intervention of beings from other worlds.

Because of its frequently bizarre manifestations, it is this dualistic version of the New Age that tends to attract most media attention. But it is only one part of the total picture, and arguably not the largest or most significant part. Many other New Agers reject such dualism, and instead adopt a monistic worldview, in which there is an essential unity between all things, both spiritual and physical. They might share a starting point with Gnosticism by understanding human alienation to be a result of people being trapped in some form of existence which inhibits the full expression of their true nature, but their answer to it is quite different. Whereas Gnostics adopted a Platonic worldview in which the human predicament was understood as a metaphysical imprisonment of the spirit in material existence, monistic New Agers frequently perceive Platonism as the root cause of the problem, and for them enlightenment comes not through escape from this material world, but very much within it, as people attune themselves to the spiritual powers that are all around them, and of which they are already themselves a part. On this view, dualism is not the answer to personal alienation, but is a part of the problem, as it tends to set up confrontations between people and the environment, between women and men, different races, and so on. On this understanding, the basic flaw in Western culture is its love affair with dualism, and the sooner that is discarded, the better. Far from being world-denying in an anti-materialistic sense (like Gnosticism), this part of the New Age tends to be strongly world-affirming.

Shirley Maclaine – whose own views are notoriously eclectic, but who is mostly representative of this monistic side of the New Age – highlights the dynamic of what is going on here, when she claims that in ancient times 'Christian Gnostics operated with New Age knowledge and thinking'.[27] In other words, the New Age provides the controlling agenda, arising from its essential character as a product of modernity, in particular the Western doctrines that materialism is a good thing, and that individual freedom and choice are the best ways to exploit material existence. Insofar as ancient

---

[27] Maclaine, *Going Within*, 30.

Gnosticism shared some aspects of that, then it can be claimed as an ally which will give an ancient image to what is in essence a contemporary movement.

The same dynamic can be discerned in the way that the New Age typically deals with ideas drawn from Eastern spirituality. Though reincarnation, for example, is popular in many New Age circles, it is altogether too simplistic to understand this merely as a form of Indian philosophy transferred to the West, for the way reincarnation is typically articulated by New Agers has only peripheral connections with either Indian metaphysics or ethics. Motivated first and foremost by values inherited from modernity, even reincarnation can be presented as a matter of individual human choice, assuming that people are here in the form they now have because they have chosen it in accordance with their own cosmic intentions, and for their ultimate spiritual development. Social psychology professor J. L. Simmons has expressed this very precisely, with his claim that 'the decision to be reborn is self-determined by each being . . . The rebirth is planned . . . Such plans include the circumstances of birth and a blueprint outline of the life to follow, so that certain experiences might provide the opportunity to learn certain lessons.'[28] Opinions of this sort have nothing at all to do with traditional Eastern spirituality: they are the product of recent Western culture, with its emphasis on personal responsibility and individual choice, and depend on the underlying philosophy of modernity, which projects an unrealistically optimistic view of human nature with no limits at all to human potential.[29]

The New Age is clearly the product of competing contemporary Western worldviews, and whenever materials from other traditions are utilized they are consistently cut loose from their original contexts and ransacked for whatever spiritual insights they may seem to offer. For that very reason, there is also a sociological side to the rise of the New Age which will help to identify other reasons for its current popularity.

One of the most unexpected places where New Age thinking has been taken seriously is in the training of top business executives.

---

[28] J. L. Simmons, *The Emerging New Age* (Santa Fe: Bear & Co., 1990), 69–70.
[29] This understanding of reincarnation also raises some frightening moral spectres: cf. my *What Is the New Age Still Saying to the Church?*, 81–119.

A management course written by two professors at Stanford University (one of the élite ivy-league universities in the USA) describes its rationale as follows:

> We look within to find our own individual self and universal source. That source has been called the inner self, the Self, the hidden mind, the divine spark, the Divine Ego, the Great I Am, God, and Essence. Some say that the very purpose of human existence is to get acquainted with your own essential qualities and express them in your daily activities. Whether it is the purpose of life or not, it is a fine definition of personal creativity: living every moment from your essence.[30]

These authors then proceed to offer advice about assorted spiritual techniques and therapies that, they claim, will put modern executives in touch with spiritual realities, including overt instructions on how to contact disembodied spirits allegedly existing in other worlds. Nor is this an isolated example: the phenomenon of New Age business courses has been well documented elsewhere.[31]

So what do ambitious business executives, homeless New Age travellers, high-profile members of the British aristocracy, and countless multitudes of visitors to New Age festivals have in common? The answer, perhaps, is deceptively simple: they are all struggling with the discontinuities of Western life at the beginning of the new millennium, the loss of power by Westerners in general, and by significant minorities in particular. In his book *The Interruption of Eternity*, Carl Raschke observed that such forms of esoteric spirituality have arisen throughout history as responses to a loss of social power and prestige. In this context, the disinherited (who do not necessarily need to be rich, but could be anywhere on the socio-economic spectrum) retreat into 'a self-enforced pariah mentality, expressed in both their contempt for legitimate authority and their creation of a closed symbolic universe which only those with the proper credentials can penetrate . . . the safekeeping of magical

---

[30] Michael Ray and Rochelle Myers, *Creativity in Business* (New York: Doubleday, 1986), 9.

[31] Cf. Rachel Storm, 'Disciples of the New Age', in *International Management* (March 1991), 42–45; Richard Roberts, 'Power and Empowerment: New Age Managers and the Dialectics of Modernity/Postmodernity', in *Religion Today* 9/3 (1994), 3–13; and my *What Is the New Age Still Saying to the Church?*, 150–173.

lore reflects a vicarious exercise of power which in reality has slipped away from them'.[32]

This can help to explain why there are so many superficial resemblances between the New Age and earlier movements such as Gnosticism, for both may be understood as responses to the break-down of the prevailing culture. Ancient Gnosticism flourished in part as a response to the collapse of the Greek worldview as it had been applied and exploited by the pragmatism of Rome, while the New Age is a reaction to the collapse of what is, in effect, the same essential worldview – this time mediated through the Renaissance, Reformation, Enlightenment and the colonialist expansion of Western nations. More than fifty years ago, Aldous Huxley argued that whenever material revelation became problematic there has been throughout the history of the West a tendency to revert to what he called 'the perennial philosophy', and search instead for an essentialist, idealist (and therefore timeless) way of understanding the meaning of life.[33] When combined with further traumas for Western culture related to rapid globalization, the spoiling of the environment and the manifest failure of the Enlightenment vision, it is obvious that for much of the twentieth century the New Age had always been a movement just waiting to happen.

## Christian Responses

Finally, we come to a brief survey of some Christian responses to the New Age. Considering the way in which the New Age has opened up the whole subject of spirituality and placed it firmly on the popular agenda, it is remarkable how few Christians have engaged with it at all. Moreover, when they have done so, they have frequently made two mistakes that have tended to undermine, rather than enhance, the Christian case.

First has been the tendency to adopt an uncritical approach which assumes that the New Age is some kind of monolithic move-ment that can be categorized rather easily. This undifferentiated approach has led some to suppose that lurking behind the New Age

---

[32] C. A. Raschke, *The Interruption of Eternity* (Chicago: Nelson-Hall, 1980), 42.
[33] A. Huxley, *The Perennial Philosophy* (New York: Harper, 1944).

is a conspiratorial attempt to undermine Western civilization as we know it.[34] But if Western civilization is collapsing, it is not as a result of any New Age conspiracy against it but because of inherent flaws in its own philosophical base. Indeed, the New Age – however inadequately – is trying to ask where we go from here, given that the inherited Enlightenment vision seems to be no longer viable. As far as I can see, there is absolutely no evidence of any New Age conspiracy to undermine democracy or whatever, and on those occasions when New Age people do use triumphalist language they are to be viewed in the same light as Christians, who similarly claim from time to time that they will 'revolutionize the world with the gospel' (and who, of course, would be strongly resistant to the notion that such optimism constitutes a devious conspiratorial attempt to undermine the social order).

Allied to this is the tendency of Christians to fail to take account of the different nuances that undoubtedly exist within the New Age. For example, Christians have often seen the New Age as an essentially occult movement. While some traditionally occult practices are undoubtedly followed by some New Agers, this is a tiny proportion of the entire movement (I would estimate that less than 10 per cent of it falls into this category). In addition, it is widely taken for granted that the New Age has a monistic worldview, whereas in reality it quite clearly has at least two worldviews, one monistic and the other strongly dualistic.[35] These two strands do not share the same heritage: the one has historical connections to a creation-based spirituality which is either pantheistic or panentheistic and which can be traced through the writings of Romantic poets such as P. B. Shelley (1792–1822), William Blake (1757–1827), and William Wordsworth (1770–1850), while the other has more in common with the overtly religious movements associated with people like Swedenborg and other eighteenth-century figures such

---

[34] For examples of this approach, see Constance Cumbey, *The Hidden Dangers of the Rainbow* (Lafayette, LA: Huntington House, 1983); Alan Morrison, *The Serpent and the Cross* (Birmingham: K & M Books, 1994).

[35] I myself failed to note this distinction in my original study of the New Age, and assumed that monism was one of its universal characteristics (*What Is the New Age Saying to the Church?* [London: HarperCollins, 1991]). For a corrective, see Paul Greer, 'The Aquarian Confusion: Conflicting Theologies of the New Age', in *Journal of Contemporary Religion* 10/2 (1995), 151–166.

as Friedrich Anton Mesmer (1734–1815), the psychic healer, or with psychics of the late nineteenth and early twentieth century, such as Blavatsky, Alice Bailey (1880–1949) and Edgar Cayce (1877–1945). To the outsider they might easily look like two entirely unrelated movements. There is certainly a significant discontinuity between them, which is a major reason why some commentators have dismissed the New Age as irrational and nonsensical. But a more productive understanding will locate these apparent contradictions in the New Age's foundational understanding of the nature of human alienation. For the alienation experienced by Western people today is not, on the whole, a cosmological or metaphysical phenomenon, but a cultural alienation. In this context, the ultimate expression of spiritual ignorance is critical scientific thinking, and it is from this that the human spirit must be set free.

This in turn highlights a further weakness in many (perhaps most) Christian responses to the New Age, which have tended to tackle it on a rational, analytical level.[36] It is not that the New Age ought not to be subjected to such criticism. Indeed, in the face of an increasingly irrational intellectual Establishment, one of the things that Christians need to bear witness to today is the fact that we are creatures of reason and, notwithstanding the exaggerated trust that our forebears placed in that, the capacity for rational understanding is one of the fundamental marks of being fully human. But to engage with the New Age only at this level is a serious mistake. For to most New Agers, this methodology is itself one of the key contributory factors to the crisis in Western culture. Using the tools of modernity to address the New Age will get nowhere, for it is by definition immune to rational criticism along these lines. Indeed, having the courage to transcend the boundaries of conventional linear Western forms of perception, and to discard the narrow confines of an over-reliance on rationalism is, for many, the ultimate expression of the kind of spirituality that will take us forward into the future. Psychology professor Marilyn Ferguson expresses this theme eloquently when she writes, 'We live what we

---

[36] An example of this approach would be Douglas Groothuis, *Unmasking the New Age* (Downers Grove, IL: InterVarsity Press, 1986); and *Confronting the New Age* (Downers Grove, IL: InterVarsity Press, 1988).

know. If we believe the universe and ourselves to be mechanical, we will live mechanically. On the other hand, if we know that we are part of an open universe, and that our minds are a matrix of reality, we will live more creatively and powerfully.'[37]

Christians will be on more secure ground when they draw attention to the moral relativism of much that is in the New Age. But in the process of making an honest assessment of the flaws in the New Age, Christians also need to be prepared to face up to the weaknesses of the church itself. Many conversations with New Agers, and my own observations and experiences, both point in the same direction, namely that, while many aspects of the New Age prescription for the ailments of today's world may be nonsensical and meaningless, its diagnosis of the disease is too accurate for comfort. Dean W. R. Inge (1860–1954) is reputed to have observed that 'A church that is married to the spirit of its age will find itself widowed in the next', and that just about sums up where the church today finds itself. Christian beliefs, spirituality and life-styles have become over-dependent on rational systems of thinking, with a consequent marginalization of the intuitional, the emotional, the relational and the numinous.[38]

There is a need to recognize those things that are right about the New Age analysis. But beyond that, there is also a requirement for a missiological engagement with the New Age that will effectively challenge some of its conclusions. It would take another book to spell out in any detail specifically what this might involve. But it would involve serious consideration of scriptural models such as that provided by Acts 17:16–34 (Paul in Athens), as well as being based on the evangelistic 'style' adopted by Jesus.[39] Identifying 'the unknown god' in today's burgeoning spiritual market place will be challenging for many Christians, and probably threatening, because it requires a confidence to move well beyond the safe boundaries of

---

[37] Ferguson, *The Aquarian Conspiracy*, 146.

[38] For more on this, see my *Faith in a Changing Culture* (London: HarperCollins, 1997).

[39] For some consideration of what this 'style' might be, see my article 'Patterns of Evangelization in Paul and Jesus: A Way Forward in the Jesus-Paul Debate?' in J. B. Green and M. M. B. Turner (eds), *Jesus of Nazareth: Lord and Christ* (Grand Rapids: Eerdmans, 1994), 281–296.

current church perceptions, which in turn is likely to open those who do it to criticism from others within the Christian community. Australians Ross Clifford and Philip Johnson are among the few genuine trail-blazers in this direction, and their book *Sacred Quest* deserves to be more widely known than it is, pointing the way forward to effective engagement with the New Age, and at the same time posing hard questions for the church that could yet lead to the emergence of a way of being Christian that will be so attuned to the realities of contemporary culture that there will be no need for New Age spiritual searchers to look any further.[40]

---

[40] Ross Clifford and Philip Johnson, *Sacred Quest* (Sutherland, NSW: Albatross, 1995)

# Chapter 3

# Ancient Gnosis for a New Millennium: Nag Hammadi and the New Age[1]

Though their place in the popular imagination has been somewhat overshadowed by the Dead Sea Scrolls, the Nag Hammadi texts were arguably one of the most significant discoveries of the twentieth century. Uncovered in upper Egypt sometime around the end of World War II by a farmer digging manure, this collection of manuscripts, produced by a Gnostic group in about AD 350 has had a profound impact not only on New Testament studies, but also more especially on the emergence of popular spirituality within the New Age. One of the first fruits of these discoveries was the publication in 1959 of the text of *The Gospel of Thomas*. It was a modest enterprise of fewer than seventy pages, with the Coptic text on one side, and an English translation facing it. The translation and the text contained critical comments, variant renditions were offered, and a scholarly apparatus for understanding them all was provided through footnotes.[2] In other words, it was a typical work of solid textual scholarship in the traditional mode. It was published simultaneously under three

---

[1]  This chapter has not previously been published. An early version of it was presented as a paper at the Exeter Colloquium on the Discovery and Significance of the Nag Hammadi Library, 3–5 September 1996, held at the University of Exeter, England, to mark the fiftieth anniversary of the discovery of the Nag Hammadi texts. In its present form, it was presented as my address as honorary president of Edinburgh Theological Society in January 1997, under the title 'Is Anything New under the Sun? Gnosticism, the New Age, and Trends in Contemporary Scholarship'.

[2]  A. Guillaumont, H-Ch Puech, G. Quispel et al., *The Gospel According to Thomas* (Leiden: E. J. Brill 1959).

different imprints: E. J. Brill in Holland, William Collins in London, and Harper Brothers in New York. Under the Brill and Collins imprints it sold a limited number of copies, but the American edition sold out almost overnight, and was subsequently reprinted many times, going on to become one of the best-selling titles in the entire Harper's religious list, with more than 100,000 copies in print. In Europe it was only scholars, libraries, and a handful of adventurous students of theology who bought this book; in the USA it was eagerly sought after by people from all walks of life. Virtually none of them could read Coptic, nor did they have any interest in textual criticism. Moreover, these people were not conventionally religious – certainly not Christian – and most of them found *Thomas* as mysterious and impenetrable after they had read it as it was before they started. Yet they bought this book, and recommended it to their friends, because they sensed that if its arcane mystical code language could be cracked it would somehow lead to a breakthrough to a new understanding of the meaning of life, which would be what the world needed to hear as the twentieth century drew to a close. Later, when in due course the entire Nag Hammadi library became available in English translation, the same publishing phenomenon repeated itself. Almost fifty thousand copies of a hardback edition sold literally overnight, followed by another eighty thousand in a paperback version, and when a new revised edition came from the presses some years later, the same thing happened again.[3] Today, *The Gospel of Thomas* even has its own home page on the World Wide Web.[4]

At that time, especially to European people, the spiritual search that was to become the New Age seemed eccentric and unbelievable, and was readily dismissed as the kind of thing that might engage rich Californians who were looking for new toys because they already had everything else – but not something that could ever have a major influence on mainstream culture. Today, all that has changed, and the search for a new spirituality that will give meaning to life in the twenty-first century is high on the agenda of the entire Western world. Moreover, today's spiritual search is not,

---

[3] J. M. Robinson (ed.), *The Nag Hammadi Library in English* (New York: Harper & Row, 1977; San Francisco: HarperCollins, rev. edn, 1988).

[4] htttp//www.epix.net/~miser17/Thomas.html

for the most part, related to religious organizations or traditional churches. Nor – contrary to some caricatures – are today's spiritual searchers a minority group of drop-outs from the mainstream. Depending on how the New Age is defined, it may not be an exaggeration to claim that its spiritual influence is now making itself felt at every level of Western culture.[5]

## Definitions

Similarities between the New Age and Gnosticism emerge even at the most fundamental level of trying to decide what each of these phenomena might consist of. We have already discussed some of the problems related to defining exactly what we might mean by the New Age, and exactly the same questions about definition have been raised in connection with Gnosticism, most notably in a recent book by Michael A. Williams, the title of which sums up the gist of his argument: *Rethinking 'Gnosticism': an argument for dismantling a dubious category*.[6] The reasons he advances for questioning the continued serviceability of the notion of 'Gnosticism' are remarkably similar to those being proposed by those who wish to dispense with the idea of the 'New Age'. Yet in spite of the obvious slipperiness of both terms, there can be no doubt that, whatever it is they represent, they do correspond with identifiable spiritual movements. In each case, a very broad definition ends up being too vague and unspecific to be of much use at all, while too exact a definition is unable to encompass the eclectic diversity which is undoubtedly a major characteristic of both phenomena. Given this similarity, there must be at least some chance that, on a phenomenological level, each of the two movements might easily shed light on the internal workings of the other – a prospect that is only enhanced by the fact that many people within the New Age trace specific historical connections not only with various spiritual and psychical movements that flourished between the 18th and early 20th

---

[5] According to Lawrence Osborn, 'New Age ideas and activities are now virtually coextensive with western culture' (*Angels of Light?* [London: Daybreak, 1992], xii).

[6] Michael A. Williams, *Rethinking 'Gnosticism': an argument for dismantling a dubious category* (Princeton NJ: Princeton University Press 1996).

centuries, but further back still to ancient Gnosticism itself. We cannot ignore the fact, however, that it is not possible to make a simple identification between the New Age and these earlier movements: in many instances, the differences are more striking than the similarities, and the New Age is undoubtedly more universal in its appeal than any or all of them.

One of the most serviceable descriptions of the New Age that I have ever had was also one of the most impressionistic, offered to me by an African-American basketball coach in San Francisco:

> Think of the New Age as a vacuum cleaner. It picks up whatever is out there, and messes it all up. So when you open the bag, you recognize all the bits and pieces that are in here – but the mixture is completely different from anything you've ever seen before, or anything you could even imagine. You probably wonder how it can all possibly belong together. The fact is, it doesn't. Those things are in there just because the vacuum cleaner happened to pick them up. If it had moved in a different direction, it would have sucked all kinds of other things in. They would look quite unlike the first collection – but they would be 'New Age' as well.

Using this model, the question 'What is the New Age?' will usefully be addressed not so much by looking at the contents of the bag, but at the machine itself, and the hand that is guiding it. We should bear in mind, of course, that talking of the New Age as a machine or a guiding hand can itself create an over-precise image, and in reality there is no one way of actually being a New Ager. It is easier to engage with particular New Age people or groups than it is to describe the entire phenomenon – and in this sense at least, it is not too different from ancient Gnosticism, which is an additional reason why it is worth comparing and contrasting the two.

We may begin with a typical New Age statement: 'So when we go within and come into alignment with our spiritual power, we come into connection with that spark of Divinity that I have mentioned before, which I call the Higher Self. Some call it the Divine Oversoul, the Divine Center, the God within, the personal interface with God . . . whatever one calls it, it is the personalization of the God Source within us.'[7]

---

[7]  Shirley Maclaine, *Going Within* (London: Bantam 1990), 83.

When that is placed alongside a typical Gnostic statement, it is immediately obvious that the two are to be located within the same overall frame of reference. For example: 'the kingdom of God is inside of you . . . when you come to know yourselves, then you will become known and you will realize that it is you who are the sons of the living Father. But if you will not know yourselves, you dwell in poverty and it is you who are that poverty.'[8]

There are of course also some differences, to which we shall return. Though the emergence of the New Age is symptomatic of some mainstream trends in Western culture, it is only recently that the world of scholarship has paid much attention to the phenomenon. Social scientists were the first to engage with it, but their work – at least in its earlier phases – was restricted by the tendency to classify the New Age as a New Religious Movement. There is certainly an overlap between these two categories, but an uncritical identification of them can only confuse rather than clarify. On the one hand, a New Religious Movement is not *per se* part of the New Age (there is actually a good deal of antagonism towards New Agers among many members of NRMs) – while on the other, the New Age itself is generally more diffuse and unstructured than the highly organized sectarianism of NRMs. The need for a more differentiated and multifaceted model is now increasingly recognized by social scientists who, whatever their shortcomings, are in any event well ahead of scholars of religion and theology, who for the most part have paid no attention at all to the New Age phenomenon, dismissing it as trendy, ephemeral and irrational, and therefore not worth serious study.

I have already suggested that the New Age is first and foremost a cultural movement, inspired by dissatisfaction with the values of modernity, and motivated by the conviction that for the human race – indeed the entire cosmos – to survive, a massive transformational shift in consciousness is required. In other words, the New Age is a response to the present crisis in modernity – in effect, a form of post-modernism projected as spirituality. Its emergence at this point in time is both a symptom of the collapse of the Enlightenment consensus, and also a driving force for social and cultural change as we look to the future. At the same time, and

---

[8]  *Gospel of Thomas* 32:25–33:5 (Logion 3).

paradoxically, it is to some extent an expression of the very forces of modernity with which it is so dissatisfied – not to mention its openness to some values that can only be labelled 'pre-modern'. Within this complex interplay of differing cultural norms, the one theme that regularly recurs is a dissatisfaction with the inherited spirituality of the West, often expressed in the form to which previous chapters have drawn attention, namely that Christianity is part of the problem, which means it cannot also be part of the solution. This explains the widespread assumption that if spirituality is to be restored to today's world, it will have to come from some other source. The nature and range of the sources regularly being consulted nowadays is quite amazing, and highlights the loss of focus in our culture. But since the primary concern is to find practical solutions that will transform our present ways of understanding and doing things, it is no surprise that any alternative paradigm which offers something different and distinctive will be of immediate potential value to the average New Age searcher. It is this concern to locate pragmatic transformational categories that explains how the New Age can hold together so many things that, on more conventional understandings, might appear incompatible and even logically contradictory and mutually self-exclusive.

## New Age and Gnosticism

In seeking to relate all this to Gnosticism, one need not look very far. To varying degrees, many New Age people would claim that their spirituality, if not identical with ancient Gnosticism, is certainly continuous with it, and is its most natural expression for the twenty-first century. There is a good deal of empirical evidence to support such a claim. For example, when New Agers express the hope that the traditions of Eastern mysticism and Western rationalism can now somehow be brought together, it is illuminating to recall the way in which Hans Jonas defined ancient Gnosticism as a meeting and mingling of precisely those two forces:

> What we do witness at the period roughly corresponding with the beginnings of Christianity is an explosion of the East. Like long-pent-up waters its force broke through the Hellenistic crust and

flooded the ancient world, flowing into the established Greek forms and filling them with their content, besides creating their own new beds. The metamorphosis of Hellenism into a religious oriental culture was set on foot.[9]

Other mainline scholars have also written of a contemporary 'rediscovery of Gnosis',[10] or 'the reclamation and renewal of the old Gnosis'.[11] In reality, though, it is not quite so straightforward. We have already referred to Shirley Maclaine's claim that in the ancient world 'Christian Gnostics operated with New Age knowledge and thinking for hundreds of years after the death of Christ'[12] – an assertion that highlights the fact that, whatever the relationship between New Age and Gnosticism may turn out to be, it is the New Age agenda, and not the Gnostic agenda, which is firmly in control. Other evidence for this tendency emerges from even a cursory reading of the journal *Gnosis*, which is one of the most successful regular publications of the New Age. Its ethos seeks to convey the impression of a strong sense of continuity with those Gnostic movements which thrived in the Roman Empire in the early years of the Christian era. Yet since its first appearance in 1985, only two issues have concerned themselves with Gnosticism in this narrow sense. More often than not, its articles are on other subjects, and if Gnosticism features at all, its mythologies are decontextualised and adapted for use within some other frame of reference.[13]

The same general trend can be discerned even among those groups who are quite deliberately committed to reconstructing ancient Gnosticism, by consciously setting out to establish worship

---

[9] Hans Jonas, *The Gnostic Religion* (Boston: Beacon, 2nd edn, 1963), 23

[10] G. Filoramo, *The History of Gnosticism* (Oxford: Blackwell, 1990), xii.

[11] Theodore Roszak, *Where the Wasteland Ends: Politics and Transcendence in Post-Industrial Society* (Garden City, NY: Doubleday, 1972), 262.

[12] Maclaine, *Going Within*, 30.

[13] The same method informs most of the essays in R. A. Segal (ed.), *The Allure of Gnosticism* (Chicago: Open Court, 1995), where the editor seeks to define a form of 'Gnosticism' which – in sharp distinction from the Nag Hammadi texts – 'need not even involve the cosmos', but 'can be entirely psychological, political, or social', combined with a radical redefinition (ancient Gnostics would surely say abandonment) of dualism itself (cf. his 'Introduction', 2–9).

centres modelled on what they imagine went on at places like the Gnostic community which produced the Nag Hammadi library. One of the most visible organized manifestations of contemporary Gnosticism is the *Ecclesia Gnostica*, based in Los Angeles and headed by Dr Stephan Hoeller, otherwise known as Bishop Tau Stephanus. This group is structured much like any regular Christian church, with services held most days of the week at the Gnostic Sanctuary on Hollywood Boulevard, and its site on the World Wide Web provides an extensive collection of lectures, liturgies, texts and other materials.[14] In addition to its own mission churches in Oregon and Utah, the *Ecclesia Gnostica* also sponsors the lay-oriented Gnostic Society, and operates seminaries in Arizona and Norway, as well as having informal connections with other Gnostic churches in the USA, and internationally in Scandinavia, Brazil, Australia, France and elsewhere. Like many other religious organizations, however, the Gnostic church is highly fragmented, and a random search for 'Gnostic church' on the World Wide Web is likely to produce in excess of two thousand sites!

The French connection is often invoked to describe the historical origin of today's Gnostic churches, tracing some kind of lineage back through secret orders such as the Rosicrucians, Martinists, Freemasons and Knights Templar, to the Cathars, and thence to the ancient Gnostic groups known from the heresiologist Irenaeus, Bishop of Lyons in the second century, and also from the Nag Hammadi texts. The gradual emergence of organized Gnostic groups in modern times can be traced through the activities of various renegade priests in the Roman Catholic Church in France during the late eighteenth and nineteenth centuries. These include Fr Pierre-Eugene-Michel Vintras, an esoteric visionary whose influence was sufficient to earn the condemnation of Pope Pius IX in 1851, and Joseph René Vilatte, a missionary who eventually became archbishop of the Old Catholic Church of America. Movements initiated by these figures, and consolidated by the work of Jules-Benoit Doinel du Val Michel (aka Tau Valentin II) led to the constitution of the French Gnostic Church in 1890. In the English-speaking world, interest in Gnosticism flourished under the patronage of the Theosophical Society (Doinel, for example,

---

received visions regarding the Gnostic church while staying at the home of Lady Caithness, a prominent British Theosophist of the day).[15] But it was not until midway through the twentieth century that the Australian-born British Gnostic Richard Powell (aka Richard, duc de Palatine) established a sacramental Gnostic church in Britain and the USA, known initially as the Pre-Nicene Gnostic Catholic Church.

Today there is a worldwide network of small, mostly independent, Gnostic churches, and at the International Gnostic Synod held in January 1997 to discuss Gnostic plans for the millennium, most countries of the developed world were represented. The Ecclesia Gnostica Mysteriorum, based in Palo Alto, California, is fairly typical of such churches. It is not without significance that a Gnostic church should locate itself in this city which is home not only to Stanford University, but is also the centre of much of the American computer industry. There is something particularly appropriate in the way high-tech industry, dominated by microprocessors, computers and robots – not to mention the implicit search for ways of creating artificial intelligence – stands alongside an overtly expressed human search for inner self-knowledge and spiritual truth. The Ecclesia Gnostica Mysteriorum advertises its purpose in the following terms: 'We teach the individual to reach the state in which gnosis can be made manifest . . . through the understanding of the rich legacy of early myths and symbolism from numerous sources . . . and through ritual, celebrating . . . archetypical acts of ceremonial communion with the timeless realities of the soul.'[16]

Gnostic worship embodying this ideal takes place every Sunday morning in a large room overlooking a shopping centre. Up to a hundred people gather, seated in chairs, and facing an elaborate altar

---

[15] According to Richard Smith, modern Gnosticism is in essence a syncretistic movement formed out of Theosophy and Jungian psychology, and has nothing at all to do with ancient Gnosticism as evidenced in, for example, the Nag Hammadi texts: cf. his article 'The Revival of Ancient Gnosis', in Segal, *Allure of Gnosticism*, 204–223.

[16] All references to this group are taken either from its own publicity materials, or from personal interviews with leaders and members of the group on different occasions during the 1990s. Cf. also Rosamonde Miller, 'The Experience of Gnosis', in Segal, *Allure of Gnosticism*, 199–203.

that is slightly raised above the main floor level, bathed in candlelight and surrounded by symbols that include flowers and peacock feathers, as well as simple figurines of ancient cult personages. The worship itself is described as a Gnostic Eucharist, at which the presiding bishop wears a simple white robe, with an attractive stole colourfully decorated with floral patterns, while other priests have plain white robes vaguely reminiscent of Christian vestments, though more obviously patterned after a classical Roman toga. There is incense, wafers and a large goblet of wine, together with much singing which is mostly harmonic chanting in a hybrid musical style somewhere between traditional Gregorian chants and the music of the ecumenical community at Taizé. In many ways, what takes place is remarkably similar to a traditional Christian mass, though there are some striking differences. For example, the bishop is a woman, as are most if not all of the priests who play a central role in the ritual. There are male priests, but their main function seems to be to hold a canopy over the altar, not unlike the *huppa* at a traditional Jewish wedding. The ritual takes place beneath this canopy, centred on the women priests and the wine of the Eucharist, all of which are conspicuously veiled. When I visited this group, Bishop Rosamonde Miller explained the significance of the veils to me as follows: 'The veils on the women and the veil on the wine symbolize the same thing as the transformation of the bread and wine. It is a veil in which the divinity, the presence of the extraordinary – Christ, God, whatever you want to call it – hides.'

The texts from Nag Hammadi feature quite prominently in this liturgy – indeed, it appears to consist of scarcely anything else but the repetition of selections from the texts, expressed in both spoken and sung form. That is not to say, however, that these modern Gnostics are trying to recreate whatever they imagine went on in ancient Gnostic communities. One striking difference is the lack of any sense of secrecy. Literally anyone can attend and take part in the Gnostic Eucharist, without any requirements to join anything or to undergo special initiation ceremonies of any kind (though several such are available for those who want them). Moreover, while there is great reverence for the Nag Hammadi texts, these are not used as a source for theology as such, and do not bear scriptural authority. Bishop Miller insisted that 'Our church has no dogmas and no beliefs. Beliefs hinder the experience of Gnosis.' Such a statement inevitably raises another question, namely what is meant by 'beliefs' – for clearly, today's Gnostics do have a belief-system in the sense of a worldview by which they make sense of things. The Ecclesia Gnostica itself publishes a list of fourteen distinctive doctrinal positions, and while it states that it 'does not require communicants to accept these teachings as a matter of belief', it goes on to admit that 'it is obvious that these teachings represent the distinctive contribution of the Gnostic tradition to religious thought, and persons functioning within the tradition would find themselves in general agreement with them'.

In this respect, Bishop Miller's avowedly non-confessional stance creates more problems than it solves. But it is certainly true that, while the myths of ancient Gnosticism are deeply respected, and ritually celebrated, they do not necessarily provide the basic structure of modern Gnostic thinking. What seems to happen is that Gnostic ideas from the past become symbols by which to explain some of modern life's mysteries, especially in relation to the discontinuities experienced on the interface between Western scientism and technology (and, behind it, the whole of Western culture) and the search for personal value and meaning. The contemporary Gnostic analysis runs roughly along the following lines:

> We are all outsiders in a meaningless world, trapped in systems and societies which create division and disharmony among people and, ultimately, prevent us from relating to the spiritual side of existence, through which alone we can discover true meaning and satisfaction. Such meaning is to be discovered by ignoring the false images of the world as we know it, and finding the common identity between our own innermost self and the ultimate spiritual power of the cosmos.

This understanding bears more than a passing resemblance to the psychology of Carl Gustav Jung – indeed, one of the founder members of the Palo Alto Gnostic church was June Singer, a life-long student of Jung, and a well-known therapist. Lance Beizer, a lawyer and another one-time priest in this group, explained his role to me as follows:

> As a Gnostic priest, I operate as an intermediary rather than a teacher. You can teach a foreign language, or that Jesus was born at a particular time and died at a certain time, and that his death has a certain kind of

meaning. But that sort of information is not the same as knowledge of what religion is, what God is, what our own society is. That is not a thing that can either be taught, or even communicated. The central idea of Gnosticism is the *gnosis kardias*, or knowledge of the heart. That is unrelated to intellectual activity: it has to do with the individual ability to perceive truth. Down at bottom, we have to make our own determinations and decisions. A *gnosis* that can be taught just isn't true *gnosis*.

By way of further explanation, Bishop Miller adds that 'In the Gnostic tradition, you don't follow what has been written. You follow what is found experientially – within yourself.' It is not surprising, then, that there is a strong connection between modern Gnosticism and psychotherapy. Jung himself found inspiration in what he knew of ancient Gnosticism, and though he was not directly one of the founders of transpersonal psychology, this is the discipline within which much of this is now coming to full expression.

## Similarities and Differences

But is this 'real Gnosticism'? In what sense is all this dependent on or derived from classical Gnostic opinions, as documented for example in the Nag Hammadi texts? Is there some genuine line of continuity that can be traced between the two phenomena? Is the modern 'revival' of Gnosticism really a rediscovery of insights long forgotten? Or is it inspired by a different, decidedly contemporary and Western agenda, which has taken over a ready-made mythology from the past in order to give itself a history, and thereby legitimate its own existence and enhance its perceived significance? In what sense are today's Gnostic communities a shadow image of the community at Nag Hammadi?

I have already hinted at my answer to those questions, and I want now to suggest that what is happening in those parts of the New Age that engage with ancient Gnostic texts (and not all New Agers do) takes its primary inspiration not from the concerns of ancient Gnostics, but from the agenda of modern New Agers. In Chapter 2, I proposed four fundamental theological compass points which may be used to explore New Age spirituality:

non-Western, first-nation, creation-centred and person-centred. Comparing ancient Gnosticism with these concerns, it is not difficult to understand how and why it should have such a wide appeal in this context.

It is, from a modern Western perspective, Eastern – or, at least, certainly not 'Western' in the classic historical sense. Moreover, within Western culture it has suffered the same fate as first-nation spiritualities. In the ideological battles of the early years of the Christian church, Gnosticism lost out and as a result was relegated to the margins as heretical and misguided. But what might the West have been like if Gnosticism had won? Would Western culture have been inspired and led by a gentler form of being, one that would have been more environmentally friendly, less aggressive and more harmonious? We shall never know, of course, but given where we find ourselves now, might it not be worth trying, to see what happens? At any rate, it is not difficult to fit Gnosticism into both of the first two categories.

When we come to the third strand, creation-centredness, then Gnosticism might appear to have fewer obvious connections here – and it is certainly in this area that ancient Gnosticism and New Age begin to pull in different directions. But within the New Age, the concern for a creation-centred spirituality tends to invoke primal understandings of the earth as spiritually alive, if not divine, and this focus – at least in its dualistic manifestation – does share with Gnosticism an interest in spiritual entities from other worlds, and a concern for elaborate mythologies, not infrequently incorporated within some kind of astrological framework. Moreover, Western esoteric movements such as Spiritualism and Theosophy provide plausible antecedents for the integration of Gnosticism and occultism, alongside elements derived from classical Eastern religions.

Finally, Gnosticism also has an obvious connection with the concerns of psychotherapy, not only through the specific commitments of Jung, but also more generally through a shared agenda of topics related to human alienation, the search for authentic identity and so on.[17]

---

[17] Probably the major thread holding together the somewhat diffuse essays collected together in Segal, *Allure of Gnosticism*, is the general assumption that ancient Gnostic myths can be universalized to become archetypal images representing the human quest for meaning and purpose.

At face value, then, Gnosticism seems to have the potential for providing the mortar that could hold together these four building blocks of New Age spirituality in some kind of coherent relationship. But is it possible to trace other more specific connections between early Gnostic communities and the New Age? As with so many questions in this area, the answer to that could be both yes and no, for while there are some obvious common elements, there are also a number of glaring discontinuities.

It is an easy and obvious remark to point out that, in sociological terms, the context in which these two movements developed, to which they were in part reacting, and which helped to shape them, is essentially one and the same.[18] Gnosticism and the New Age both arose in the context of cultural collapse and change. But it is not merely a question of history repeating itself, because there are some fundamental differences in the way that the basic problem of human existence is addressed. Gnosticism and the New Age both see people as trapped in some form of existence which is alien to their true nature. For ancient Gnostics, this was an essentially metaphysical imprisonment of the spirit, and was the work of the Demiurge. In other words, the Gnostic approach began with a reaffirmation of an essentially Platonic worldview. The New Age, however, generally takes an opposing viewpoint, and regards Platonism in all its forms as the root cause of today's problems. Paradoxically, though, it is not difficult to find what look like New Age restatements of the Gnostic view. Though she generally aligns herself with a monistic worldview, Shirley Maclaine, for instance, echoes dualistic Gnostic teaching when she states that 'Birth into the physical is . . . a limitation of the spirit, and death of the physical is the return of the spirit to its proper domain'.[19] The same understanding is elaborated even more emphatically by Sir George Trevelyan who, in his book *Operation Redemption*, makes a specific connection between New Age and ancient Gnosticism, claiming the familiar historical lineage through the Knights Templar, the Cathars and Albigenses, Rosicrucianism and Freemasonry. Within

---

[18] On the social influences impinging on ancient Gnosticism, see Henry A. Green, *The Economic and Social Origins of Gnosticism* (Atlanta: Scholars Press, 1985).
[19] Maclaine, *Going Within*, 210–211.

that stream of consciousness, he argues that there is a spiritual hierarchy in which humanity stands as the 'tenth plane of being', presently suffering 'a kind of death, a descent into the prison or tomb of the body and personality and the five senses . . . a drastic limitation of the free-ranging spirit'.[20] Furthermore, he defines redemption from this condition in terms of liberation from the demiurgal power which enslaves us, so that we develop into 'a species no longer merely earth-bound, but capable of sense-free thinking that can consciously enter the realms of spirit and work with the great angelic beings'. Trevelyan quotes with approval an entry in a friend's journal: 'Understand these things, for man's purpose now is to move out into his divine Destiny and away from the disintegrating mooring to an old and dying world.'[21]

This kind of metaphysical dualism is indeed essentially the same as is found in ancient Gnosticism.[22] Within the New Age context, it leads not only to the philosophical reflections of people like Trevelyan, but also to concern with channelling messages from spirit guides and extraterrestrials, and speculating about lost worlds and aliens, or ancient legends of Druids and Arthurian Britain. On this understanding, the answer to the human predicament can only be found in some other world that is beyond this one, and salvation can only come as messages are received here from that other world. Or can it? Shirley Maclaine gives a different spin to all this when she claims that 'A great awakening is taking place. Individuals across the world are tapping in *to their internal power* to understand who they are and using that knowledge to elevate their lives and their circumstances to a higher octave of happiness and productivity.'[23] Again, though, it is not difficult to find similar statements among the ancient Gnostics. Monoimus bears comparison here, with the

---

[20]　See George Trevelyan, *Operation Redemption: A Vision of Hope in an Age of Turmoil* (Walpole, NH: Stillpoint Publishing, 1985), esp. 19–20, 65–66, 151, 181
[21]　Trevelyan, *Operation Redemption*, 23, 27, 70, 75, 153, 161, 179.
[22]　Not all New Agers would take this line, however. Indeed, perhaps a majority would hold a far more linear view of time and history, eagerly anticipating progress to a new way of being, which will appear here in this world. Trevelyan represents a strand of the New Age which would seek salvation in a separation from matter as intrinsically evil, but the more common view is that salvation will only come as we discover new ways to be at one with the material world.
[23]　Maclaine, *Going Within*, 56–57; emphasis added.

advice to 'Abandon the search for God and the creation and other matters of a similar sort. Look for him by taking yourself as the starting point. Learn who it is within you who makes everything his own and says, "My God, my mind, my thought, my soul, my body." Learn the sources of sorrow, joy, love, hate . . . If you carefully investigate these matters you will find him in yourself.'[24]

The New Age, however, introduces a different twist into all this, arising from its essential character as a product of modernity, and its affirmation of key Enlightenment beliefs about materialism and individualism. Shirley Maclaine is again a helpful guide to this: 'the body is basically an aggregate of universal particles that the Higher Self has sculpted to experience a physical existence and truly fulfill its purpose for that life-time. When that mission is completed, the particles disperse and become part of the Earth (on which the life was experienced), which in time disperses the particles back to the universe.'[25] Two things are noteworthy about this. First, though there is clearly a notion of reincarnation in here that would not be out of place either in Gnosticism or Indian philosophy, its nature and quality is related neither to Gnostic metaphysics nor Hindu ethics. On the contrary – as was pointed out in Chapter 2 – reincarnation in the New Age is here perceived as a matter of individual human choice.

Far from being imprisoned in matter by alien and hostile forces, we are here by our own free choice, and the subsequent experience is one that has positive, not negative, repercussions for our ultimate spiritual development. Reference was made earlier to the ontology of Professor J. L. Simmons, but he takes things a step further by proposing that this personal control over our own destiny is in no way diminished even once material incarnation has taken place: 'We create the realities we experience . . . The universe ultimately gives us what we ask for . . . Since we construct our own lives, it is false and misleading to blame others for what we are experiencing . . . The buck stops with us. And change is in our own hands.'[26]

This New Age understanding obviously entails a very exalted view of humanity. Its emphasis on the need for individuals to be

---

[24] Hippolytus, *Ref.* 8.15.1–2.
[25] Maclaine, *Going Within*, 136.
[26] J. L. Simmons, *The Emerging New Age* (Santa Fe: Bear & Co., 1990), 83.

their own teacher allows for no limits to human potential, and offers a totally optimistic view of human nature. It all operates in a very different world from the determinism of classical Gnostic thought. For the New Age, cosmic forces are not deterministic, but give access to new forms of free choice.[27] What we have here is a utilization of two key themes that have been obtained from what in historical terms would have been different sources: a metaphysical dualism with belief in a spirit world, and a notion of reincarnation. But in each case the concepts have been torn away from their original ideological foundations and rebuilt into a thought system that not only incorporates, but is dominated by the individualistic philosophy of modernity. This also explains why, far from being world-denying in an anti-materialistic sense, the New Age is generally strongly world-affirming, in terms of lifestyle as well as cosmology. For the true Gnostic, Shirley Maclaine's view that 'When the mission is completed, the particles [of spirit in humanity] disperse and become part of the earth' would not bring ultimate liberty, but further enslavement – whereas for her, the earth itself actually becomes a means of salvation, taking benevolent initiatives on behalf of the spirits entrusted to it.

At this point her view is difficult, if not impossible, to reconcile with other statements she herself makes even in the same book, and this obvious tension highlights what we have already identified as one of the major paradoxes in the entire New Age philosophy. For on the one hand there is this strongly dualistic and patriarchal understanding, rooted in movements such as Rosicrucianism and Theosophy, while on the other, there is a strong creation-based spirituality which is either pantheistic or panentheistic, with historical connections to the Romantic poets and the American Transcendentalists, not to mention other more contemporary links with the eco-feminist revival of Wicca, and even to some aspects of more mainstream feminist theology. On this view, salvation comes not from outside, but from within. There is no other world, and what we can see is all that we have. If there is to be redemption, then

---

[26] Cf. for example the way in which the New Age eagerly adapts old-fashioned mediumship into New Age channelling, so that messages from the unknown become not predictive or directive, but a means of providing opportunities for individuals to make better-informed choices about their own lifestyle and destiny.

it will come from our own engagement with ourselves and our ability to live at peace with the rest of creation. Far from dualism being the answer to the human predicament, dualism is itself the problem – not only metaphysical dualism which enslaves us to concepts of some other world, but political dualisms, gender dualisms, economic and social dualisms. Moreover, critical scientific thinking as developed in Western culture is perceived as a major weapon in the arsenal of such dualisms, for this is what provided the tools with which to articulate some of the most damaging dualisms of all: namely, the elevation of the left brain over against the right brain, analysis against intuition, men against women, Caucasians against other races, and so on.

In this context, it is no surprise to find yet other motifs from ancient Gnosticism surfacing in New Age debates. For example, the Gnostic interest in androgyny can be expressed as an embodiment of 'the conquest of all duality'.[28] Shirley Maclaine speaks of her 'higher self' as 'an androgynous being with long arms and the kindest face I had ever seen'[29] – though she typically defines this not as androgynous in the strict sense, but as a rediscovery of the feminine: 'When the feminine Goddess in each of us is recognized, the spiritualization of the physical plane will be accomplished . . . Then we will have spiritualized the material and materialized the spiritual. And we will be expressing ourselves for what we truly are – androgynous, a perfect balance.'[30] She would find it harder to accept the judgment of *The Gospel of Thomas*, that all will be well only when the feminine becomes masculine![31]

It is precisely because of such discontinuities within the New Age that many commentators struggle to identify the nature of the movement. Not a few give up, concluding that the whole thing is romanticized nonsense, and the way that even a single author can be both dualistic and non-dualistic at the same time is evidence of that. But another way of looking at it is to locate these apparent contradictions in the New Age's understanding of the nature of human alienation, which I have already suggested is a cultural alienation, not a cosmological or metaphysical one, and that

---

[28] Filoramo, *History of Gnosticism*, 61.
[29] Maclaine, *Going Within*, 87.
[30] Maclaine, *Going Within*, 196–7.
[31] *Gospel of Thomas* 51:19–25 (Logion 114).

within this frame of reference the ultimate expression of spiritual ignorance is critical scientific thinking.[32] It is not the Gnostic Demiurge who here arrogantly claims, 'It is I who am god; there is none apart from me'[33] – but Western thought and culture. This is the major source of human oppression, and if we can transcend it, we can become new people. Since we are interconnected with all other things, not only can we undergo personal transformation, but we will also be able to recreate the entire cosmos in the process. This helps to explain why rational criticism of the New Age generally cuts no ice with those who are committed to this kind of spiritual search – because to be able to transcend the boundaries of conventional linear Western forms of perception, and to discard the narrow confines of rationalism are, for many, the ultimate expressions of New Age spirituality.

## Wider Connections

We have previously noticed the tendency within Western culture to revert to an essentialist worldview whenever material revelation (whether religious or not) becomes problematic, and Carl Raschke's study of Gnosticism was referred to in the previous chapter in this connection. One of his major contributions to this debate was the proposal that, throughout its history, Gnosticism 'represents an ideology peculiar to the latter stages in the demise of the ruling-classes', through which an anxious and disinherited élite responds to the loss of social power and prestige, and in the process 'gradually surrenders its leadership functions and devotes its energies to letters and learning' as a way of somehow convincing itself that it still has something not accessible to more ordinary mortals.[34] It is perfectly plausible to argue that both modern

---

[32] Contrary to the view of S. A. McKnight, that modernity itself is 'Gnostic' in nature: cf. his article 'Eric Voegelin and the Changing Perspective on the Gnostic Features of Modernity', in Segal, *Allure of Gnosticism*, 136–146. This emphasis on cultural alienation rather than introspective personal estrangement is a further significant factor that distances the New Age proper from much of the modern Gnostic movement.

[33] *Hypostasis of the Archons* 86:30.

[34] C. A. Raschke, *The Interruption of Eternity* (Chicago: Nelson-Hall, 1980), 42.

adaptations of Gnosticism and the New Age itself are part of the renewed search for a new aristocratic spirituality, which will enable the élites to hold on to power. No doubt this is at least part of the reason for the popularity of New Age techniques in business training, and the consequent emergence of a new managerial aristocracy. But it is by no means the only place where this is happening, and it is worth asking whether the same ideological concerns are not part of the agenda of much contemporary study of ancient Gnosticism itself. No-one can fail to notice the gulf that has emerged between European understandings of some Nag Hammadi texts and North American appraisals of the very same materials in relation to mainstream biblical and theological scholarship. Taken as a whole, North American scholarship has a predilection for regarding texts such as *Thomas* as independent witnesses to the Jesus tradition, and therefore of at least equal value to the canonical gospels in the search for authentic teachings of Jesus.[35] European scholars, on the other hand, in an unusual show of unity that transcends all shades of theological opinion, are more inclined to regard the canonical materials as the primary sources and the Gnostic texts as somehow derivative or secondary. Could it be that the key issue here is not historical and textual judgements as such, but a strong ideological division between these two scholarly communities that itself is not unrelated to the New Age postulate that humanity today is imprisoned not by metaphysical realities, but by inherited cultural norms? Europeans in this debate generally still trust the objective status of the familiar tools of scholarly analysis developed under the Enlightenment influence, whereas their North American counterparts have no hesitation in declaring the end of even the possibility of value-free understandings. Writing in his own Festschrift (itself surely an incredibly post-modern thing to do!), Helmut Koester deconstructs the historical-critical method of studying the Bible as being 'a hermeneutical tool for the liberation from conservative prejudice and from the power of ecclesiastical and political institutions', and goes on to argue for what he regards as a more appropriate method based on the quest for 'political and

---

[35] The most high-profile manifestation of this trend is no doubt to be located in the work of the Jesus Seminar: cf. R. W. Funk and R. W. Hoover, *Five Gospels, One Jesus: What Did Jesus Really Say?* (Sonoma, CA: Polebridge, 1992).

religious renewal . . . inspired by the search for equality, freedom and justice' in the context of the 'comprehensive political perspective' of today's world.[36] At a time when some systematic theologians are also attempting to redefine Christianity as a 'neotranscendentalist, pluralistic, social Trinitarian, universalist pantheism embedded in a soft epistemology'[37] (all of them ideals that can easily be documented through New Age sources) are we not faced with the intriguing possibility that the contemporary Gnostic lineage may not be located exclusively – or even primarily – within some sections of the New Age, but could be just as deeply embedded in some mainstream trends of theological scholarship? This is not the time or place to develop this particular question further. But the mere fact that it is worth asking at all only serves to reinforce the view that the current resurgence of interest in Gnosticism, whether in the New Age or elsewhere, is the product of contemporary angst in the face of a collapsing culture, and is part of the search for post-modern meaning within Western civilization rather than any kind of conscious return to either the values or, ultimately, the worldview of the sort of ancient Gnosticism represented by the texts from Nag Hammadi.

---

[37] Cf. B. A. Pearson (ed.), *The Future of Early Christianity* (Minneapolis: Fortress Press, 1991), 474–476.

[38] N. Smart and S. Konstantine, *Christian Systematic Theology* (London: Marshall Pickering, 1991), 441.

# Chapter 4

# Christianity and the Environment[1]

## Introduction

Though the New Age is far from being one monolithic entity, concern for the environment is common to just about every section of today's popular spiritual search. Since the continuing good health of the planet is essential for human well-being, this is hardly surprising – and, though there is nothing like a consensus about what should be done about it, there is widespread agreement that the earth is in worse shape than it ought to be. Ever since the first stirring of environmental concern back in the 1960s, Christians have been given a hard time by ecological activists. For many, the influential and oft-quoted statement by Lynn White Jr says all that needs to be said about the way Christian faith relates to environmental issues:

> Christianity in absolute contrast to ancient paganism and Asia's religions . . . not only established a dualism of man [sic] and nature but also insisted that it is God's will that man exploit nature . . . Christianity bears a huge burden of guilt . . . We shall continue to have a worsening ecological crisis until we reject the Christian axiom that nature has no reason for existence except to serve man.[2]

[1] The substance of this chapter was delivered in the University of Dundee as part two of the 1997 Margaret Harris Lecture in Religion, in response to part one, which was a presentation by Sir Jonathon Porritt on Christian culpability for the environmental crisis.

[2] 'The Historical Roots of our Ecological Crisis', *Science* 155 (10 March 1967), 1203–1207.

In the intervening decades it has come to be widely assumed that, if there is a solution to the ecological crisis somewhere, it is unlikely to have any connection with Christianity. It may come from a classical monistic worldview – Buddhism, perhaps – but more likely, it will emerge from a conglomerate 'designer' spirituality of the kind that is typified by the New Age. It is argued that just about anything would be more environmentally friendly than Christianity, and with the encouragement of scientists who are also New Agers, it is now almost taken for granted that unless we learn to reverence the earth as divine, or semi-divine, there will be no incentive for us not to spoil things.[3] In theory, at least, people who think whales and dolphins may in another life have been their own relatives are less likely to kill them.

Christians may question – with some justice – the understanding of history and scripture proposed by people who argue in this way.[4] But, as with much else for which Christianity is being blamed today, there is an element of truth underlying these claims. It is undeniable that some of the leading figures of the Industrial Revolution were motivated not only by the Calvinist work ethic, but also by the conviction that they had some sort of divinely endowed right to exploit the world and its resources. However, like most of the aspects of contemporary culture examined in preceding chapters, this matter also is not quite as straightforward as it can be made to seem. For one thing, this analysis of our present ecological predicament is far too simple an understanding of what is, on any reckoning, an exceedingly complex topic. Anyone who believes that today's environmental crisis can be reduced to just one single cause – whether it be overpopulation, economic growth, the modern scientific method, dualism, patriarchy, Christianity or,

---

[3] Cf. Rupert Sheldrake, *A New Science of Life* (London: Paladin, 1980); James Lovelock, *Gaia: a New Look at Life on Earth* (New York: OUP, 1979); Fritjof Capra, *The Turning Point* (New York: Simon & Schuster, 1982), esp. 431–466. Lovelock explicitly denied that he was putting forward a 'spiritual' understanding when he defined the earth as a single living entity to which he gave the name Gaia. But his use of the name of a Greek goddess inevitably meant he would be understood in that way.

[4] For a scathing critique along these lines, cf. James Barr, 'Man and Nature: The Ecological Controversy and the Old Testament', *Bulletin of the John Rylands Library* 55 (1972), 9–32.

indeed, any other religious or philosophical system – is naïve and simplistic. Moreover, the question of Christianity's alleged complicity in environmental exploitation needs to be addressed in a more subtle way, by asking two quite separate, though obviously not unconnected, questions. One relates to the behaviour of actual people who have called themselves Christians, while the other relates to the intrinsic values and principles of Christian belief as evidenced in the Bible, the teaching of Jesus and the mainstream of the Christian tradition down through the centuries. In relation to the first, there can be absolutely no question that empirically, Western Christians have played their part in the ongoing emergence of today's crisis – though equally, even as we admit that, it must be insisted that the facts do not show them to have been single-handedly responsible, for atheistic communists, and even Asian Buddhists, have also done their fair share. But it is also the case that, insofar as Western Christians have encouraged exploitational use of the natural world, they have done so not as Christians, but first and foremost as Westerners. For in common with the rest of Western culture over the last five hundred years or so, they have explicitly denied some key Christian teachings, while embracing with unwarranted enthusiasm the worldview we now refer to as modernity. In particular, I want to suggest here that Christians today are dealing with the fallout of a theological and cultural time-bomb left by their forebears' uncritical acceptance of the materialist values of the Enlightenment, with its pretentious optimism about human potential, and which in turn spawned a self-centred individualism that inevitably led to a reduction in the sense of responsibility towards other people and for the wider environment.

## Historical Background

The emergence of modernity as the dominating mindset of Western culture led to changes in social processes and individual self-awareness of such magnitude that human relationships with the natural environment could hardly fail to be profoundly affected. From a theological point of view, one of the key factors in this was the rejection of divine revelation as any kind of guide to the meaning of life, and its replacement by the belief that human reason should henceforth be the only true locus of moral and spiritual meaning and purpose. This moral redefinition of human behaviour, inspired by a utilitarian perspective which put personal feelings and satisfaction in the place of any external sanctions, inevitably played a significant role in the marginalization of nature. Once the meaning of life has become something essentially interior to the human psyche, then relationships with nature are intrinsically without purpose, except insofar as they serve the overriding need for individual human happiness. On such an understanding, the whole point of human life becomes self-fulfilment through material acquisition, rather than moral goodness or spiritual fulfilment. This in turn encouraged the development of a rampant consumerism, both justifying and encouraging the exploitation not only of the physical environment, but also of other non-Western people.

In the wider historical perspective it is clear that all urban civilizations of all times have always created environmental pollution. In Old Testament times the Fertile Crescent that stretched from the rivers Tigris and Euphrates on the Persian Gulf westwards to Egypt was able to sustain very significant and powerful nations. But overgrazing and deforestation led to soil erosion so serious that even by the time of the great ancient empires of Assyria and Babylon, enormous resources were required just to keep the irrigation channels free of silt. Eventually nature won, the canals filled up, commerce was impossible, and political power moved westwards until the discovery of oil in more recent times. A similar story can be told of ancient Rome, whose streets were so polluted by the ancient equivalent of burger stalls that in the middle of the first century AD the Latin writer Seneca reported positive health benefits whenever he left it: 'As soon as I escaped from the oppressive atmosphere of the city and that dreadful aroma of reeking cooked-meat stalls, which when trundled about belch forth a mixture of soot and all the offensive smells they have accumulated, I immediately felt an improvement in my health.'[5] But in ancient times, such ecological abuse was always a localized phenomenon.

---

[5] Seneca, *Epistulae Morales* 104.6. I am grateful to Morton Gauld, my colleague in the University of Aberdeen, for helping me to identify this quotation, and kindly supplying the translation which I have included here.

Today, industrialization, increasing mobility and the growth of global economies have magnified and speeded up this process, which explains why it is only the expansion of relatively recent Western empires that has elevated the matter to crisis proportions.

If we add to this change of attitudes the further development of science and technology, exploited through industrialization, the Cartesian mechanistic understanding of the world, and the later contribution of the theory of evolution, with its implicit notion that some life forms are more advanced, and therefore more 'valuable', than others, then it was entirely predictable that a very powerful brew indeed would be produced, that was almost designed for the express purpose of dissolving the very fabric of the natural world and reconstituting it so as to serve the perceived happiness of people – white, Western and mostly male people, that is.

In this changed cultural climate, what the Christian tradition had previously regarded as the gift of God to be nurtured and sustained now came to be understood as the property of people. During the centuries in which this worldview was evolving, those who sought to resist these trends were in a minority, and they themselves eventually succumbed to more powerful cultural forces. The medieval monasteries, for example, had from their inception been communities with a clearly articulated concern for the world of nature, first of all in the sense that they were contemplative orders whose key purpose was to reflect on God's handiwork in the natural world, but in addition they also self-consciously regarded themselves as the guardians of a model of sustainable farming that was rooted in a spirituality of nature which regarded land as a gift from God, and therefore a precious resource to be nurtured and preserved. On the whole, the medieval church threw its not inconsiderable weight behind this understanding, and imposed powerful sanctions against the buying and selling of land for personal gain, the lending of money for interest, and so on. These were all values that should have set the church on a collision course with the emerging socio-economic system, had it not been for the fact that by the new definitions of what constituted a market economy, church leaders found themselves redefined as major land-owners. In this new climate, even the monastic communities saw the possibility of new powers falling within their grasp and, by replacing people with sheep, ended up making their own contribution to that redefinition of the relationship between people and nature which came to characterize the worldview of modernity. Orders like the Franciscans and Dominicans resisted such moves, but the Reformation provided an opportunity for their influence to be much reduced, and when its own emphasis on the autonomous individual as the centre of all things was coupled with the theological characterization of nature – both human and physical – as irredeemably sinful, the vestiges of opposition to a wholesale despiritualisation of the natural world collapsed. In the emerging theology, sacred spaces and places became at best of secondary importance as compared to personal belief, and the locus even of divine revelation was firmly fixed as being in the life of individual people.

Historically, it is not difficult to argue that Christian theology by itself was not responsible for the despiritualisation of nature, though equally it is hard to deny that some central aspects of Protestant opinion lent themselves rather easily to the support of the emerging secular culture. Taking a longer historical view, though, it is clear that it was the denial and rejection of the traditional Christian view of nature as the sphere of God's working, and its replacement by an instrumental view of nature, that helped create an atmosphere that in the ensuing centuries would be conducive to the wholesale exploitation of the environment. The precise relationship between Reformation, Enlightenment and the development of science and technology is too complex to be addressed here and to do so would take us well beyond our major focus. But the outcome of this unholy alliance can hardly be disputed for, as a result of it, many Western Christians came to adopt three basic assumptions about the environment, all of which were a denial of the historic Christian worldview. These assumptions were, first, that creation exists solely for the benefit of humans, and can therefore be exploited at will regardless of the cost; second, that God is essentially transcendent, quite separate from creation and no longer involved in it; and third, that all physical matter is sinful in comparison to the spirit (which, following classic Greek philosophical dogma, could also be equated with the powers of reason).

These assumptions found clear expression in the work of many pioneers of Western science. It was the Christian Sir Isaac Newton (1642–1727), for example, who replaced the traditional biblical belief that God directly sustains and is everywhere present in the world of nature, with a mechanistic view of fixed 'laws of nature' which assumed that all that happens can be explained in terms of cause and effect – and above all that, though God created the world, God is now completely removed and separate from it.[6] In the process, reverence for the mystery of the universe was replaced by human reason. Such thinking distanced God from creation, and reinforced the view that human nature must therefore be totally and irredeemably fallen and sinful. God might have created the universe, but because of human sin God had abandoned interest in it – and henceforth it would be up to people to manipulate nature in whatever ways might be beneficial to themselves. This attitude has prevailed for the greater part of the last three hundred years, if not always with the explicit approval of Christianity, then certainly with no effective opposition from it. Once more, we return here to a theme already familiar from previous chapters: as a result of their wholesale uncritical adoption of the worldview of modernity, Christians now find themselves seriously undermined as believable advocates of any kind of spiritual resolution to our present predicament.

## Searching for Biblical Insights

There is insufficient space here for a detailed exegesis of all the relevant biblical texts, but it will still be worthwhile to spend some time reflecting in a more discursive fashion on the overall thrust of the Bible's message. Christians do well to remember that if others believe that the Bible endorses the indiscriminate exploitation of nature, that is not usually the outcome of a first-hand acquaintance with the relevant texts. The Bible is not required reading for environmental activists, and if such people have understood its message in this way, then they have been given that impression by people who do read the Bible, and have told them – whether through words or lifestyles – that this is what it says. In point of fact, the Bible is more serviceable in the present circumstances than even some Christians believe.

It at least begins its analysis of the human predicament in the right place. The simple stories of its opening chapters depict the sort of

---

[6] Cf. Lesslie Newbigin, *Foolishness to the Greeks* (Geneva: WCC, 1986), 21ff. and *passim*.

world we would all like to believe in (Genesis 1:1–2:25). This is a world in which plants, animals, and people coexist in peaceful harmony, where the careful ecological balance of nature operates to near-perfection, exploitation is a word that has not yet entered the vocabulary of the human race, and the cosmos is under control because it is in the hands of its loving divine Creator and Sustainer. Everyone and everything occupies their God-appointed place in this idyllic scene where each part of the cosmos can function as it was intended and reach its own full potential in the process. This is the world of our dreams – the world as it once was, perhaps, and certainly the world as we would like to see it again. Then into this world comes the possibility of disaster, as the human couple living in the garden of perfect ecological balance and personal spiritual openness are presented with a series of choices. Could they perhaps improve on things by taking matters into their own hands? Is it necessary for them to live in harmony with nature and in dependence on the God who stands behind it all? As the story unfolds, they decide to go it alone and, instead of continuing to enjoy a harmonious connection with their own environment, things start going wrong (Genesis 3:1–24). Not only is the careful balance of nature disrupted, but relationships with their own kind collapse, as one of their sons murders his own brother (Genesis 4:8–16). Even in the face of such abject misery, human self-confidence knows no limits, as the remaining stories of the early chapters of Genesis make clear (Genesis 5:1–11:32).

In dealing with this kind of story, we should not allow ourselves to be sidetracked into arguing about how it can be integrated with 'scientific' accounts of such things. Nor is it likely to be morally productive to argue about the literary genre of the narratives. To imagine that these are the central issues of the early chapters of Genesis is to allow ourselves to be lulled into a sense of false security in our own wisdom, while missing the striking message that the stories themselves are intended to convey: human self-sufficiency, self-confidence, and self-indulgence lead to disaster. When expressed in those terms, no contemporary thinker could improve on this ancient story as a comment on the last few centuries of Western history.

Based on what we find in the Bible, the essential ingredients of Christian belief about the natural world can be summarized under four main propositions:

- *Christian belief is theocentric*: this is why it is legitimate to critique the Christian tradition by reference to its own intrinsic values. It is possible even for those within the tradition to corrupt its intrinsic message, and the continuing existence of a strong prophetic strain of understanding shows how easily, and how often, that has been done.

- *People have a particular value*: this is why Christians can never treat the environment as a free-standing issue. Where nature is exploited, people are invariably being oppressed as well. The anguish of people and the suffering of nature are two sides of the same coin and it is irresponsible, if not impossible, to deal with one without also addressing the other.

- *People are accountable*: things happen not according to some irresistible cosmic accident, but in relation to moral choices made by humankind.

- *The Christ-story is central*: it affirms God's concern for and blessing of the natural world, and further depicts a view of God which is relational (three persons in Trinity), thereby underlining the importance of mutuality in human relationships with one another, and with the environment.

Having set this frame of reference, we now need to take a closer look at some aspects of the Bible's message. In Genesis 2:15–20 Adam was instructed to take care of the garden in which he lived, and the animals are said to have been created to provide companionship for him. In the event, no suitable partner could actually be found from among their number, but by even raising the question in that way the story obviously assumes a relationship of interdependence between Adam and nature. This is not quite a relationship of equality, as he was also invited to name the creatures, which suggests some sense of control over or responsibility for them – a notion which is spelled out in the prior statement that God's intention for humankind was to be 'in our image, according to our likeness' and 'have dominion over the fish of the sea, and over the birds of the air, and over the cattle, and over all the wild animals of the earth, and over every creeping thing that creeps upon the earth' (Genesis 1:26,28). The meaning of that statement is crucial to any biblical perspective on Christian care for the environment, and two terms in particular are central: 'dominion', and being in God's 'image'.[7]

The Hebrew word translated 'dominion' occurs in other Old Testament contexts (e.g. Psalm 8:6–8), and always conveys a sense of power and authority, usually associated with the rule of kings. But if the rule of the king was in some way the model for human 'dominion' over creation, therein lies a significant clue to the understanding of this term within its ancient scriptural context. For elsewhere in the Torah, two principles are laid down to determine how a king ought to rule: 'neither exalting himself above other members of the community nor turning aside from the command-ment [of God]' (Deuteronomy 17:20). In terms of social organization, the king was to be a leader among equals, not a despot; while on an ideological level, everything the king did was to be rooted in devotion to God. In practice this meant the king should be just, loving and merciful in dealing with other citizens, just as God had been with the nation (cf. Psalm 72:12–14). Kings often failed to match this high ideal, and in both respects – the ideal and the reality – there is a worthwhile parallel with the Bible's position on environmental responsibility.[8]

In this context, exercising 'dominion' was clearly intended to involve the care and sustenance of the earth. This conclusion is

---

[7] This of course is the main passage which has allegedly encouraged Christians to exploit the environment with impunity: 'If you want to find one text of com-pounded horror which will guarantee that the relationship of man [sic] to nature can only be destruction . . . which will explain all of the destruction and all of the despoliation accomplished by western man for at least these 2000 years, then you do not have to look any further than this ghastly, calamitous text' (Ian L. McHarg, *Design with Nature* [New York: Natural History Press, 1969], 26). Such an opinion is not only textually questionable, it is also historically untrue: Christian-ity existed for at least 1500 years before the rise of science and technology, and the beginning of the present crisis!

[8] And one that is not undermined by the fact that the Genesis passages about dominion were addressed to small agrarian peasant communities, whose 'dominion' only extended to flocks and fields, with practical concerns like keeping wolves at bay. Our context is certainly larger – and different – but the principles remain the same.

underlined by the complementary affirmation that humankind is 'in the image of God'. Though there has been much debate on the matter, the consensus of opinion seems to be that this phrase designates people as, in the broadest sense, 'God's representatives': in the way that they behave and relate to the world round about them, humans should imitate God.[9] The idea that human behaviour should be modelled on the known characteristics of God is of course central to the whole of biblical morality. Emil Brunner summed it up concisely when he described it as 'the science of human conduct as it is determined by divine conduct',[10] and when that is applied in the sphere of environmental care it can only mean that, in the same way as God is just, loving, and merciful, these qualities should also characterize human relationships with the natural world order.

If Genesis 1 gives people considerable status in the order of creation, then Genesis 2 expresses a different, but no less significant, perception about the natural balance of things. In this passage, humankind is described as created from the dust of the earth, emphasizing that people are directly related to the environment in the most material sense imaginable, and in spite of their own exaggerated estimates of their status, are themselves an intrinsic part of nature. Other texts say the same thing. If Psalm 8 makes people only 'a little lower than God' (Psalm 8:5), then Psalm 144 describes them as 'a breath . . . a passing shadow' (Psalm 144:3–4).[11] In Psalm 104 there is a lengthy discussion of how God created and sustains every part of the environment and every living creature. In this kaleidoscope of vitality, humankind is 'just another figure in the landscape', and the whole psalm expresses a far-reaching view of the interdependence of different parts of the natural world.[12]

Many other passages in the Bible refer to human responsibilities for the well-being of the environment, most such references being the more impressive because they are generally coincidental to the

---

[9] For a succinct account of the linguistic and other arguments, see G. Wenham, *Genesis 1–15* (Waco: Word, 1987), 29ff.

[10] E. Brunner, *The Divine Imperative* (London: Lutterworth Press, 1937), 86.

[11] See also Psalm 49:12; Isaiah 40:6–7; Job 38–41.

[12] J. Austin Baker, in H. Montefiore (ed.), *Man and Nature* (London: Collins, 1975), 88.

main thrust of the various texts. For example, the laws relating to Sabbath years and the Jubilee endow land itself with the right to rest and renewal (Leviticus 25), while more than one passage justifies Sabbath observance by reference to the right of animals to rest (Exodus 20:10; 23:12). In Deuteronomy, the natural world is accorded intrinsic rights that supersede even the most pressing human needs (20:19), while the same book also concerns itself with the correct disposal of litter (23:13). Elsewhere, the care of a shepherd for the flock is legendary – and clearly genuine, for it can be used as a picture of God's love for people (Psalm 23:1,6; Isaiah 40:11; Luke 15:4–7, etc.). Concern and consideration for animals is reflected in other Old Testament passages (e.g. Deuteronomy 25:4; Exodus 23:19; Deuteronomy 22:6), and the same theme is re-emphasized through the attitudes of Jesus in the New Testament (Luke 14:5; 13:15,16; Matthew 11:30, etc.). In Jeremiah 12:10–11, the prophet expressed the fear that human greed and irresponsibility may destroy the fertility of the land, while Isaiah (11:1–9) had no hesitation in including all creation – humanity, animals, and the wider environmental infrastructure – in the coming golden age.[13]

There is, then, a good deal of evidence to suggest that in the Bible human beings are thought of both as a part of nature, and also responsible to God for it. Moreover, it is not difficult to identify passages showing that the natural world is of great value to God, and that animals and plants have certain rights that are quite independent of the interests of humans.

## Immanence, Incarnation, and Blessing

Does the Bible also encourage Christians to go further and affirm that God is continuously present in creation, or that an experience of

---

[13] Cf. also Romans 8:18–24; Isaiah 65:25; Revelation 5:13–14, and the rebuke given by God to Jonah in response to his displeasure at the sparing of the city of Nineveh: 'Should I not be concerned about Nineveh, that great city, in which there are more than a hundred and twenty thousand persons who do not know their right hand from their left, and also many animals?' (Jonah 4:11). The point is, that even if God was going to look foolish for overlooking the wrongdoing of the adult population, was it not right that special consideration should at least be given to the children and animals.

nature can also be an experience of God? In the Old Testament, Psalm 139 reflects a belief that God's spirit is in and sustains the whole of creation in a way that is quite different from either the scientific theories of people like Newton or the dualistic outlook permeating classical Greek philosophy and inherited by much traditional Christian thinking. Paul presents a similar understanding in Romans 8:18–23 (cf. also Colossians 1:15–20),[14] and the underlying worldview of such passages seems to regard every part of creation (humans, animals and the wider environment) as interrelated, awaiting a time when all will be fully liberated from their suffering. Paul's thinking is certainly not dualistic here: on the contrary, he celebrates the physical nature of people and cosmos and, through Christ, considers the physical to be infused by the presence of God.[15]

Theologically, all this is rooted in the incarnation which, if it means anything at all, must put a question mark against any notion that God is completely separate from creation, or that physical creation is sinful *per se* (John 1:1–4,14). By becoming a child and being involved in all the processes of birth, God endorsed human creativity at its most materialistic level, for birth and death are the two points at which humankind most obviously shares the same capacities and qualities as every other creature within the natural world. The irony – and, for many, the unacceptability – of this way of understanding Christ was soon noticed in the early church. Even then (long before the Enlightenment!) there were those who found it impossible to accept such a close identification between God and nature – a tendency which engendered the Docetic and Gnostic groups of the early Christian centuries,[16] and which encouraged subsequent generations to conclude that all physical matter is sinful in comparison to the spirit or the powers of reason.

---

[14] Cf. also the fact that the same terms (*ruach/pneuma*) are used to designate the Spirit of God in both creation and redemption.

[15] Cf. also the statement attributed to him in Acts 17:28, backed up by a quotation from the Greek poet Epimenides: 'God . . . is not far from each one of us. For "in him we live and move and have our being" . . .'

[16] The fact that Luke goes to such lengths to emphasize that Jesus was actually God not only from birth, but even from conception, suggests this discomfort with God's endorsement of materiality originated at a very early period in the church's life (Luke 1:46–55; 2:29–32,14–48, etc.).

This takes us finally, then, to the proposition that beliefs about the fallenness of humanity and nature, based on the story of the Fall in Genesis 3:1–24, inevitably lead to negative and exploitational attitudes toward the environment. Like many other claims reviewed here, this one is both true and false. It is a matter of historical fact that, when combined with a Greek-inspired matter/spirit dualism, the Fall story has been interpreted in ways that actively discouraged Christians from regarding nature, or even their own bodies, as relating in any way to spiritual wholeness. The medieval theologian Thomas à Kempis put it succinctly when he observed, 'Every time I go into creation, I withdraw from God . . . nothing in creation can compare with the Creator . . . unless a man is freed from dependence on creatures, he cannot turn freely to the things of God . . . while Nature is often misled, grace trusts in God and cannot be deceived.'[17] There is plenty of evidence to show the disabling effects of a dualism which separates the material from the spiritual, identifying the one with sin and the other with holiness. Many people have been incorrigibly damaged by the mistaken belief that the human body, society, and even the earth itself is totally corrupt and unregenerate. Women in particular have suffered from being defined purely in terms of their sexuality and this, when coupled with a dualistic understanding of creativity, has directly contributed to their exploitation. Christians have frequently ignored or played down the role of nature as part of God's revelation. They have failed to take seriously statements such as Genesis 1:31, where God pronounces the earth to be 'good', and makes statements of blessing and affirmation over the physical creation.

In the hands of Matthew Fox, these deficiencies have become the starting point for a comprehensive redefinition of much of Christian theology.[18] Fox has argued powerfully in favour of what he calls creation-centred spirituality, as distinct from a fall-redemption paradigm. Fox believes that the Western church,

---

[17]  Thomas à Kempis, *The Imitation of Christ* 3.31, 'On Forsaking Creatures to find the Creator'. Translation from Leo Sherley-Price, *The Imitation of Christ: A New Translation* (Harmondsworth: Penguin, 1952), 133–134.

[18]  For accounts of Fox's views, see Matthew Fox, *Whee! We, Wee All the Way Home* (Santa Fe: Bear & Co., 1981); *Original Blessing* (Santa Fe: Bear & Co., 1983);

dominated by male chauvinists with a highly developed individualistic sense of sin and guilt, has lost touch with its spiritual roots, which in turn has led to many Christians having dysfunctional personalities, incapable of being in tune either with themselves and their own sexuality or the deep spiritual realities that lie at the heart of the universe. A negative attitude towards our bodies and the environment is, he contends, the root cause of many of today's social and environmental problems.[19] In his view, the blame for all this can be placed squarely with Augustine (354–430), whose articulation of the concept of original sin led to a *de facto* neglect, if not actual rejection, of any sort of creation-based theology in favour of a fall-redemption model.

For Fox, the creation-centred model assumes the goodness of creation and of human nature, as rooted in God, whereas fall-redemption regards people and nature as intrinsically alienated from God. The starting points are therefore different, and whereas creation-centred spirituality promotes a holistic vision in which nature is a channel of salvation, fall-redemption dualism fosters an unhealthy alienation between people and nature, and between the physical and the spiritual and rational sides of human nature itself.

---

*(continued) The Coming of the Cosmic Christ* (San Francisco: Harper, 1988); 'Spirituality for a New Era', in Duncan S. Ferguson (ed.), *New Age Spirituality* (Louisville, KY: Westminster/John Knox Press, 1993), 196–219; and *Confessions* (San Francisco: HarperCollins, 1996). For critical responses, see Andrew Deeter Dreitcer, 'A New Creation', in *The Way* 29/1 (1989), 4–12; Ted Peters, *The Cosmic Self* (San Francisco: Harper, 1991), 120–131; Jane E. Strohl, 'The Matthew Fox Phenomenon', in *Word and World* 8 (winter 1988), 42–47; M. Brearley, 'Matthew Fox: Creation Spirituality for the Aquarian Age', in *Christian Jewish Relations* 22/2 (1989), 37–49; C. Noble, 'Matthew Fox's Cosmic Christ – A Critical Response', in *Crux* 27 (1991), 21–29; Richard J. Bauckham, 'The New Age Theology of Matthew Fox: A Christian Theological Response', in *Anvil* 13/2 (1996), 115–126; Lawrence Osborn, 'A Fox Hunter's guide to Creation Spirituality', in A. Walker (ed.), *Different Gospels* (London: SPCK, 1993), 155–172; also my article 'Matthew Fox', in Trevor A. Hart (ed.), *The Dictionary of Historical Theology* (Carlisle: Paternoster Press, forthcoming).

[19] Capra (*Turning Point*, 21) provides a useful checklist of the kind of assumptions on which traditional Western attitudes (influenced by Christianity) have been based. He characterizes this culture as Masculine, Demanding, Aggressive, Competitive, Rational, and Analytic – contrasting sharply with the new paradigm which he believes we now need, described as Feminine, Contractive, Responsive, Co-operative, Intuitive, and Synthesizing.

What he believes has happened in terms of the bigger environmental picture is that the negative self-image inculcated by fall-redemption theology was projected onto the world at large, and thereby provided a theological basis for ecological exploitation. Insofar as there is an 'original sin', Fox wants to identify it with this kind of dualism. By contrast, creation-centred spirituality begins with 'original blessing', in which nature is good and wholeness derives from rediscovering the interconnectedness between all things, which in turn will lead to an affirmation of diversity, in people as well as in nature, which celebrates plurality over against all destructive dualisms. In his extensive writings, Fox has argued that this is actually the authentic Christian position as taught by Jesus – and because the historic Jesus of Nazareth is also to be identified with the 'cosmic Christ', this wisdom can actually be found everywhere. In the course of arguing for all this, he proposes that the original creation-centred tradition can be traced throughout Christian history and, though it was displaced from centre-stage by the fall-redemption model, it survived in an attenuated form especially through the insights of medieval mystics such as Hildegard of Bingen (1098–1179), Mechthild of Magdeburg (1212–80), Meister Eckhart (1260–1327), St Francis of Assisi (1182–1226), St John of the Cross (1542–91), Teresa of Avila (1515–82), Julian of Norwich (1342 to c. 1416), and others. He then links this with his belief that mysticism is the heart of all true spirituality, which means that the same insights and underlying theology can be found in other religious traditions, notably those which in the past have been victimized by the imperialistic dualism of fall-redemption thinking and attitudes. Combining all these forces into a 'deep ecumenism' which also encompasses the work of mystical scientists such as Brian Swimme, Fritjof Capra, Rupert Sheldrake and Wendell Berry, will not only destroy dualism in all its forms (science/religion, women/men, East/West, spirituality/social justice and so on), but will also create the possibility of a new paradigm founded on 'panentheism' ('everything is in God and God is in everything') – classical theism then being relegated to the margins as a product of fall-redemption dualism.

Even from this brief summary, it will be obvious that Fox is one of those people who imagines things on the grand scale, and his thinking embraces an appropriately varied and broadly based collection of material that ranges over the entire spectrum of world spirituality. As such, it is not difficult to pick holes in specific aspects of his arguments, and that has been where most of his critics have focused their attention. Because of his swashbuckling style, he sets himself up as an easy target, which is unfortunate because much of the underlying argument is articulating key questions with which the church needs to engage. Who could not resonate with many of his criticisms of the way in which the devaluation of creation and creativity has led to the marginalization and oppression of significant groups of people all around the world? Moreover, he has the kind of innovative and transformational intent that is all too often lacking from theological debate and analysis, and the way in which he seeks to integrate theology with other disciplines, such as science and psychology, is an exciting model in itself. No one can question his commitment to the search for new perspectives that will somehow build bridges of understanding between the inherited Christian tradition and the emerging spirituality of post-modern culture. I must confess that I find myself temperamentally attracted by his writings – perhaps because his theological style is quite similar to my own. But having said that, I also find myself concluding that his questions are considerably more useful than his answers, and with a bit more rigorous discipline in his work he could have placed his questions where they certainly belong, in the centre of any debate about the future of Christian theology and the emerging culture.[20]

It is perhaps stating the obvious to say that Fox is his own worst enemy. His unfortunate tendency to try to rewrite history so that all the bad guys look like his caricature of Augustine, and all the good guys sound like Matthew Fox, has enabled serious theologians to ignore him too easily.[21] Though he has published his own editions

---

[20] Much the same might be said regarding the debate about 'post-evangelicalism' inaugurated by Dave Tomlinson, which actually has many similarities to Fox's work, though coming from a very different theological tradition: cf. D. Tomlinson, *The Post-Evangelicals* (London: Triangle, 1995); Graham Cray et al., *The Post-Evangelical Debate* (London: Triangle, 1997); David Hilborn, *Picking up the Pieces: Can Evangelicals Adapt to Contemporary Culture?* (London: Hodder & Stoughton, 1997).

[21] Cf. Rosemary Radford Ruether, 'Matthew Fox and Creation Spirituality: Strengths and Weaknesses', in *Catholic World* (July/August, 1990), 168–172; Barbara Newman, 'Romancing the Past: A Critical Look at Matthew Fox and the Medieval "Creation Mystics" ', in *Touchstone* 5 (1992), 5–10.

of the writings of medieval mystics in the course of putting forward his case, these translations are widely regarded by historical scholars as deeply flawed. For example, he simply omits huge chunks of the work of Hildegard, and mistranslates portions of Eckhart. He uses similar tactics when dealing with biblical texts, imposing meanings on them without any supporting argumentation or evidence. Moreover, his analysis of the tensions between an emphasis on creation spirituality and an understanding of fall-redemption is too simplistic: Augustine was a good deal more sophisticated and nuanced in his thinking than Fox allows him to be, while Aquinas (one of Fox's heroes) certainly espoused dualism. Even the medieval mystics, who undoubtedly emphasized the creation-centred tradition, all operated within the framework of a fall-redemption paradigm, which itself suggests that the two perspectives are not necessarily mutually exclusive within Christian thought, but have a more complex relationship with one another. His intellectual method is also regularly undisciplined and lacking in self-critical awareness. For example, he everywhere complains that Western Christianity is individualistic and anthropocentric (as distinct from being ecological or cosmological) – yet his own focus is itself highly individualistic, concerned as it is with personal fulfilment, happiness and the achievement of ecstasy through mystical experiences. And though he professes to hate dualism, in his book *Original Blessing* he provides his own dualistic analysis of the entire Christian tradition, classifying people and movements according to the categories of creation-centred versus fall-redemption paradigms, and even awarding star ratings to key historical figures, depending on how they score!

Some Christians also wish to question his theological stance on the grounds that he can at times seem to be moving towards a kind of New Age worldview, though in my opinion a far more significant criticism relates to his overall *naïveté* about sin, which he identifies with patriarchy and dualism, and regards therefore as a relatively recent phenomenon in terms of cosmic history. This allows him to propose that 'being natural' through participation in traditions ostensibly untouched by dualism will automatically lead to human perfection and the restoration of ecological balance (hence his emphasis on rituals such as shamanic drumming, sweat lodges, vision quests and so on, as contributions towards the healing of the earth). But the historical reality is that in most societies where the 'natural' has prevailed over the rational, innocent victims have repeatedly suffered precisely the kinds of personal violation that Fox finds so disturbing in today's Western culture. Moreover, though he regularly refers to the plight of the marginalized, his thinking actually has remarkably little to say to those who are oppressed, despite his attempt to claim liberation theology as part of the same movement. Though panentheism is not strictly speaking a monistic worldview, at the end of the day it seems to share monism's perennial weakness in being incapable of providing either a moral understanding or a resolution of some of our culture's most pressing problems.

In order to engage with all this in a constructive manner, however, we need to be quite clear about what we mean by fallenness. If the Fall is conceived in a hierarchical sense, as a tumble from spiritual perfection to material sinfulness, then of course it is not difficult to conclude that whatever is physical must be second-rate and unsatisfactory – the world of nature included. But is this what the biblical idea of the Fall is really about? Given the starting point of the Genesis stories – unity and harmony between women and men, between people and God, and between people and the natural world – surely the Fall is most naturally understood as the breaking of relationships. Fox is correct when he proposes that it is only a self-centred Western individualism that could regard sin exclusively in terms of a corruption of human nature. But the Bible writers take a much broader view than that – not least Paul, who envisages the whole of creation not only suffering from the fact of fallenness, but sharing in the ultimate salvation that is to be effected through Christ. By ignoring or playing down this aspect of biblical thought, Fox's argument is inadequate and, ultimately, misleading. In particular (and notwithstanding his claims to the contrary), it leads to a diminishing of the connection between environmental exploitation and the oppression of people.

In his enthusiasm for disposing of all dualism, Fox draws a false antithesis between the belief that things are in a mess (which, after all, is what the fall-redemption paradigm tries to address) and the belief that God created things good. Consequently, he is unrealistic about sin, especially in the context of the marginalized and oppressed whose primary experience is not of sinning but of being sinned-against.[22] Alongside this, we find an unrealistic optimism that assumes people not only have the ability to make right choices, but will actually choose to do so. History shows that, left to our own devices, we typically make wrong choices, and no amount of positive thinking, intuition or mystical experiences seems to make much difference. On any account, the fall-redemption paradigm is more useful here, with its acknowledgment of God's grace not only in creation but also in the life-death-resurrection of Jesus and the gift of the Spirit. It is hard to avoid the conclusion that Fox's worldview is ultimately deeply influenced by the very same self-sufficient Western individualism that he claims to be opposing.

Any spirituality which regards the created world and our own part in it solely as a backdrop for personal salvation has an inadequate understanding of sin, and consequently a deviant view of salvation, and insofar as the Western tradition has often seemed to be saying something like that, Fox is right to criticize it.[23] His own emphasis on environmental blessing begins promisingly enough, and enables him to feel more comfortable with the birth of Jesus than most Western Christians (who in practice are often covert Docetists, unable to cope with incarnation except by seeing it as a necessary step on the way to atonement). On the other hand, the way he plays down sin as both a subjective and objective fact means he is unable to make much sense out of Jesus' death, resurrection, and the gift of the Spirit. For if there is nothing to be redeemed from, it must all have been unnecessary anyway, and the New Testament's claim that, through the totality of his incarnation, Jesus

---

[22] Kathy Galloway reasonably asks, 'What does original blessing mean for those people who need a concept of original sin with its concomitant deliverance to deal with their deepest experience, which is of original hurt?' ('The Whole Earth Shall Cry Glory', *Coracle* 3/2 [1989], 18). One critic goes so far as to describe Fox's ideology as 'a potential new Holocaust' (Margaret Brearley, 'Matthew Fox: Creation Spirituality for the Aquarian Age', *Christian Jewish Relations* 22 [1989], 37–49). That seems to me to be too strong a statement, but when Fox observes that 'Fall/redemption ideologies help to keep the poor poor' (*Original Blessing*, 267) he is only telling half the story. Creation-centred spirituality is just as capable of engendering exploitation and injustice, not least because of its affinities with New Age thinking and the effective absence of any concept of God's grace.

[23] Cf. also Robert Murray, 'The Bible on God's World and Our Place in It', *Christian Jewish Relations* 22 (1989), 50–60.

brings healing and new life to the whole of creation by liberating it from the effects of sin, makes no sense at all.

Fox's dilemma is real enough, as he struggles to deal with biblical statements about divine transcendence and immanence, a paradox which he resolves by trying to have it both ways, in effect by avoiding the issue and speaking instead of 'panentheism'. But the concept of 'relatedness' is a better one with which to sum up a biblical theology of the environment.[24] 'Dominion' in Genesis 1:28 includes the active promotion of harmony and peace (*shalom*) not only between humankind and nature, but also between people. The environmental crisis cannot easily be separated from issues of gender, race, economics and other aspects of our broken world. The Bible does not support narrowly dualistic understandings of creation, the exploitation of animals and the environment by humans, or a belief that God is uninvolved in creation. On the contrary, Christians are called to be realistic about the fallenness of the cosmos, while being active agents in the process of recreation. Effective environmental action needs to be rooted in deep communion with God, recognizing our responsibility not only to nature, but to the rest of humankind as we continue to suffer from the consequences of cosmic fallenness, while bearing testimony to the fact that redemption is at hand.

---

[24] Cf. Wesley Carr, *Manifold Wisdom* (London: SPCK, 1991), 111–134. Dorothee Soelle uses similar terminology in her stimulating book *To Work and to Love* (Philadelphia: Fortress Press, 1984): 'To love God's good earth is to know about the hunger and exploitation of those who share the earth with us . . . Affirmations of beauty lack truth if they exclude the vast majority of our brothers and sisters. They are false praises, mere abstractions that are isolated from reality.' But her understanding of fallenness as 'a rise in human development . . . making our own choices, leaving the commanding father who wants to keep his trees for himself along with the womb of our mother . . .' (74) leaves her in a similar place to Fox, with no effective way of addressing – still less resolving – the challenges that she so eloquently identifies.

Chapter 5

# The Death of Diana, Princess of Wales: Missiological Lessons for the Churches[1]

## Introduction

From the moment she married into the British royal family, Diana, Princess of Wales, was always in the public spotlight. At first she was merely admired as one of the rich and beautiful people, but then as the fairytale dream evaporated and the drama of her real-life struggles, both with herself and her family relationships, unfolded in the public arena, she was embraced into the hearts not only of her own nation, but by people throughout the world who identified with her quest to find meaning and fulfilment in life. In the closing decade of the twentieth century, the ups and downs of her life became a powerful reflection of the experience of many others: full of potential, eager to do good, infused with genuine compassion, but beaten by the system and left wounded by the wayside, wondering if and how the pieces might ever be put together again. By the time she died in the early hours of Sunday 31 August 1997, the suffering she had endured, her newly found personal happiness with Dodi al-Fayedh, and her much-vaunted determination to stand alongside the disadvantaged and the marginalized seemed to reflect more than just Diana's personal story. Britain was still enjoying the wave of political euphoria that had followed the election of a new government only three months previously, and the princess's emergence into new

---

[1]  An expanded and revised version of an essay that first appeared in Chris Sugden (ed.), *Death of a Princess* (London: Silverfish, 1998), 29–48.

life was an appropriate symbol for the mood of the nation at that time. It seemed as if she had given us all a tantalizing glimpse of what the world could be like if only we were kinder and more compassionate, even in the midst of much insecurity. It was inevitable that her death would stir people at the deepest levels of the human psyche, for in a real sense she was a symbol of that combination of brokenness and healing which touches all our lives.[2] Even so, few of us were quite prepared for the amazing expressions of public anguish that lasted for several weeks after her death, and indeed still continue in many different forms not only in Britain but all over the world.

This was not the first time Britain had seen such outpourings of mass grief, and there are any number of historical precedents to which one can point, both ancient and modern. One can look as far back as the public response to the murder of Archbishop Thomas Becket in Canterbury (1170), while in the nineteenth century, the deaths of the Duke of Wellington (1852) and William Gladstone (1898) were both marked by outpourings of mass public grief. Early twentieth-century examples of the impact of tragedy on the national consciousness can be seen in the death of Queen Victoria in 1901, and then in the way the end of the Great War in 1918 started an annual national ritual that still continues to this day in the observance of Armistice Day each November.[3] It is tempting to regard the responses to Diana's death as merely the most recent example of this recurring phenomenon. But there are many aspects of it which are different, and significantly so. For what happened during September 1997 was part of an emerging pattern of devotional practice within British culture whose

---

[2]  She has been usefully compared with 'imaginary friends', performing much the same function as characters in TV soaps, or even the saints in traditional Christian spirituality, though her archetypal significance, perhaps because of the pre-millennial timing of her death, is not fully explained by such an image. Cf. Douglas J. Davies, 'Popular Reaction to the Death of Princess Diana', *Expository Times* 109/6 (1997–98), 173–176.

[3]  The common thread running through all these examples, and also present in Diana's death, is that, in their different ways, these people and events represented the nation's own self-image at the time. In the case of Gladstone, people even wrote books of poems expressing their grief, in much the same way as mourners left written messages for Diana.

development can be traced over the previous two decades in public responses to (among others) the sinking of the *Herald of Free Enterprise* in 1983, the disaster at the Hillsborough sports stadium in 1989 which left many football supporters dead, and the shooting of a whole class of schoolchildren at Dunblane Primary School in 1996 – not to mention the growing trend toward the spontaneous creation of shrines at the scenes of road accidents on all our major highways. I want to suggest that what took place following Diana's death, far from being an anomalous expression of a maverick spirituality, was actually a pivotal moment in the evolution of a new popular spirituality within Western culture.

If that is a correct understanding, it will demand some reappraisal of the secularization thesis embraced uncritically by much contemporary sociology of religion.[4] It will also, however – and this is my main purpose here – present a significant challenge to Christians in relation to the mission of the church in the contemporary world. To expand on this, I propose first to high-light some key aspects of this emerging popular spirituality, before moving on to comment briefly on the wider cultural context in which it is taking place, particularly in relation to the perceived shift from modernity to post-modernity, and the status of conventional religion. Finally, I will offer some comments on what it might mean for Christian mission, and the task of the church in the twenty-first century.

---

[4] The secularization thesis is well represented by scholars such as Bryan Wilson and Steve Bruce, while others such as David Martin, Grace Davie and Peter Berger have expressed less confidence in it. Cf. Bryan R. Wilson, *Religion in Secular Society: A sociological Comment* (Harmondsworth: Penguin, 1969); Steve Bruce, *Religion in Modern Britain* (Oxford: OUP, 1995); David Martin, *The Dilemmas of Contemporary Religion* (Oxford: Blackwell, 1978); *Tongues of Fire* (Oxford: Blackwell, 1990); Grace Davie, *Religion in Britain since 1945* (Oxford: Blackwell, 1994); Peter Berger, *The Sacred Canopy* (New York: Doubleday, 1967). For recent discussions and overview, see Jeffrey K. Hadden, 'Challenging Secularization Theory', in Anthony Giddens (ed.), *Sociology: Introductory Readings* (Cambridge: Polity Press, 1997); Julie F. Scott, 'The Truth is Out There: The Renewal of the Western Religious Consciousness', in *Scottish Journal of Religious Studies* 18/2 (1997), 115–127; Peter L. Berger (ed.), *The Desecularization of the World* (Washington DC: Ethics & Public Policy Center, 1999).

## The Nature of Popular Spirituality[5]

There are two fundamental frames of reference within which we can begin to understand what happened following Diana's death. First, and most visibly, when people went into the streets and open spaces to mark their grief, they were engaged in a form of pilgrimage. Watching events as they unfolded on television was, however, a more accessible prospect for some people, and I believe this can best be understood as a kind of vigil. Many people of course did both. The central focus of this chapter, though, is on the public displays of anguish.

Recent discussion of pilgrimage is characterized on the one hand by those who seek to understand it in the context of the established social structures[6] and, on the other, by those who prefer to see it as a more eclectic phenomenon.[7] Paradoxically, the Diana experience lends some support to both these perceptions, while also challenging them both and suggesting that pilgrimage in the post-modern world may be an even more diffuse phenomenon than was previously imagined. Several aspects are particularly note-worthy here.

In their pioneering work, anthropologists Victor and Edith Turner sought to understand pilgrimage by relating it to traditional rites of passage, emphasizing the themes of separation (leaving

---

[5] I am not here proposing to engage with what constitutes an appropriate defini-tion of 'spirituality'. The literature is vast – and growing – and opinions incredibly diverse. For a recent innovative account from a Christian perspective, see Maria Harris and Gabriel Moran, *Reshaping Christian Education: Conversations on Contemporary Practice* (Louisville, KY: Westminster/John Knox Press, 1998). The responses to Diana's death clearly qualify as 'spiritual' even on a minimal definition such as that promulgated by the UK government's Department for Education and Employment: 'The valuing of the non-material aspects of life, and intimations of an enduring reality.'

[6] Either challenging the social *status quo*, as in Victor Turner, *Process, Performance and Pilgrimage* (New Delhi: Concept Publishing, 1979); Victor Turner and Edith Turner, *Image and Pilgrimage in Christian Culture* (Oxford: Blackwell, 1978); or upholding social conventions, as in Emile Durkheim, *The Elementary Forms of the Religious Life* (London: Allen & Unwin, 1964; originally in French, 1912).

[7] Notably John Eade and Michael Sallnow, *Contesting the Sacred* (London: Routledge, 1991). For an informative collection of case studies, cf. Ian Reader and Tony Walter (eds), *Pilgrimage in Popular Culture* (London: Macmillan, 1993).

home), liminality (the journey, visit to the shrine, transforming encounter with the sacred), followed by reincorporation (going home with a new perspective). Those who joined in the mass out-pourings of grief following Diana's death clearly had a strong urge to be there, wherever 'there' might have been in any particular locality. They were experiencing what Durkheim called 'collective effervescence', and which the Turners identify somewhat differently as the creation of 'communitas' – something that, however it be described, clearly plays a key role in all forms of Christian pilgrimage.[8] But there was one crucial difference. For whereas today's Christian pilgrims tend to move out of the world into the safe spaces of like-minded people,[9] all the recent examples of mass grieving have been more like medieval pilgrimages, with people *leaving* the safe spaces of family and home, to go into the more dangerous space of the world.[10]

This fact alone raises important missiological questions, for those locations that were regarded as safe spaces where the search for new meaning might most effectively be pursued were not the traditional

---

[8] I am including here Protestant 'pilgrimages' to events like Spring Harvest (in Britain), or the mass gatherings of the Promise Keepers (for men only, mostly in the USA), as well as traditional Roman Catholic pilgrimages to places like Lourdes or Santiago de Compostela. As Reader and Walter (*Pilgrimage in Popular Culture*) show, similar features are found in pilgrimages of many religious traditions, and even in visits to supposedly 'secular' places such as battlegrounds or the sites of other historic events. Visits by Christians to the Holy Land, while containing elements of pilgrimage in relation to particular sites, are more accurately described as a specialized form of tourism. Interestingly, in the light of the Diana tragedy, Durkheim proposed that 'collective effervescence' generally emerges 'under the influence of some great collective shock' (*Elementary Forms of the Religious Life*, 210; see in general his exposition in the section 209–215).

[9] Cf. Gwen Kennedy Neville's observation, based on an analysis of North American Protestant practices: 'The actual repeated journey made by the Protestant pilgrim is not one of going out as in the classical pilgrimage but one of going back periodically as a way of escaping the individuation and depersonalization experienced as a member of a scattered, mobile, and often anonymous urban industrial society' (Gwen Kennedy Neville, *Kinship and Pilgrimage: Rituals of Reunion in American Protestant Culture* [New York: Oxford University Press, 1987], 20).

[10] On different styles of pilgrimage, see Victor W. Turner and Edith Turner, *Image and Pilgrimage in Christian Culture: Anthropological Perspectives* (New York: Columbia University Press, 1978).

sacred places of Western spirituality (churches). On the whole, they were public spaces that were transformed into sacred space, sacralized not by the rituals of religiously authorized persons, but by becoming almost a spatial extension of the interior spirituality of the mass of people who visited them. In central London, parks and other open spaces functioned in this way, while elsewhere it was often shopping malls and council offices. In some ways, this was no surprise, for there was already a strong pilgrimage tradition attached to Diana, and perhaps it was natural for people to grieve in the same places as they would have expected to see her, bearing the same gifts in death as they had done in life.

In that light, the fact that people did not, on the whole, go to churches, need not by itself be so unusual. But there can be no doubt that the preference for the sacralizing of new spaces was in large measure the natural outcome of a growing conviction within our culture generally, that religious institutions have lost sight of the spiritual, and therefore people need to take responsibility for their own personal quest for meaning. It is also significant that people preferred to confront their pain in the most dangerous space of all – the street, the very place where she met her death, and previously had been hunted by the paparazzi – rather than retreating to 'safer' surroundings. Underwriting this was an implied questioning of the value of the pre-packaged answers to tragedy that are often given by the representatives of organized religion, and a willingness to engage with the big issues that suggests a greater spiritual maturity in the population at large than conventionally religious people generally allow. In the process, we witnessed the emergence of a self-consciously do-it-yourself pilgrimage style, with little concern for whether people were following recognized cultural rules or formally sanctioned procedures, if only because there were no inherited models for doing this kind of thing. Inevitably, a number of the unwritten rules of British culture were broken, but in such a way as to rewrite the nature of the cultural conventions which will now be passed on to future generations. People wept openly in the streets, they threw flowers at Diana's coffin, they prayed in parks and in shopping centres, and they not only exposed their young children to the tragedy, but adopted their insights in seeking for resolution.

These and other similar features can only be described as significantly counter-cultural.[11]

In addition to these general characteristics, a number of other features also emerged as having special significance, not only in the aftermath of Diana's death, but also in the context of the 1996 Dunblane shootings – a coincidence which encourages me to propose that what we have seen is more than a merely fortuitous product of unexpected circumstances, and in fact provides evidence of some crucial shifts in the character of popular spirituality, indeed in the nature of our culture.[12]

### Spontaneity

A key feature in both these episodes was the emergence of a spontaneous, creation-centred spirituality, a phrase which I am choosing carefully here, for it does seem to me that the questions raised by Matthew Fox, and already discussed in the last chapter, have a direct relevance to this topic. There was certainly a concern to uncover a spirituality that would be rooted in the reality of the human condition as part of the cosmos, rather than one embodied in the inherited patterns of the rationality of Western culture. Indeed, the dominance of this rationality within our culture was widely regarded as a significant factor in the sequence of cause-and-effect leading to both these tragedies. By contrast, the

---

[11] Pilgrimage generally involves counter-cultural activities, of course, whether it be experimentation with different worship styles or whatever. But in conventional pilgrimage contexts, this experimentation is owned, and therefore controlled and restricted, by religious authorities. This is what gives plausibility to the arguments of both Durkheim and the Turners. But what happens when no one is in control? That is what took place in the aftermath of Diana's death, and the outcome was not just a different way of doing the same things, but the emergence of a different paradigm which actually questioned which things were needing to be done anyway, including – significantly – the role of the British royal family.

[12] Unlike the contributors to Digby Anderson and Peter Mullen (eds), *Faking It: The Sentimentalization of Modern Society*, (London: Social Affairs Unit, 1998), I regard this cultural shift as spiritually and morally neutral in itself. It could of course become pathogenic but, as I suggest below, there are significant redemptive elements within it, and the church's engagement with these might well determine the ultimate course which it takes.

materials used in the construction of pilgrim shrines were all strongly creation-centred in the most literal sense, with flowers, flames, and other natural materials, building and elaborating on the locus of the shrines themselves (which were almost entirely out of doors). It is tempting to see here evidence of some tension between the serious search for spiritual meaning that was happening on the streets, and the usual ways in which Christians deal with such matters, if not the actual way in which the church related to these specific tragedies.[13]

Was this an example of the cultural tensions described by George Ritzer in his 1993 book, *The McDonaldization of Society*?[14] In comparison with the evident ability of the spontaneous, do-it-yourself spirituality of the street to speak to the human condition, and provide useful vehicles for the expression of emotions of all kinds, did the inherited Western Christian ways of handling crisis look too much like what Ritzer might call 'McDoctrine' – a spiritual fast food of proof-texts and clichés that (like their culinary equivalent) might seem filling and fattening in the normal flow of everyday life (at least for those accustomed to such a diet), but which in the larger context of cosmic tragedy appeared, at best, to be irrelevant and simplistic?

Again, this can be related back to precedents in Diana's life, for she had often been portrayed as disenchanted with the Western rationalized tradition which she inherited, and which in turn had victimized her through its unyielding protocol, undergirded by appeals to some notion of universal reason. In struggling with these

---

[13] The church's response was, predictably, very diverse. In Dunblane, for example, the local churches played a key role in the healing process, and one that continued long after the initial trauma passed – just as they did in Liverpool following the 1989 Hillsborough disaster. But a surprising number of the letters received by the Dunblane community were from fundamentalist and charismatic Christians who either linked the massacre to some kind of subversive plot within society, or implied that the children had 'paid the price' for some real or imaginary transgressions by their forebears – and therefore, the tragedy was in some sense the will of God. Similar responses surfaced after Diana's death, from Christians who made a simplistic connection between her tragic end and what they regarded as her immoral lifestyle, while others regarded her demise as an outcome of her friendship with the Muslim Dodi al-Fayedh.

[14] George Ritzer, *The McDonaldization of Society* (Thousand Oaks, CA: Pine Forge Press, 1993).

opposing ways of being, she herself had regularly indulged in forms of spontaneous, do-it-yourself spirituality and, like many of her mourners, she sought to create a relevant personal path by utilizing ancient ingredients in the reinvention of a meaningful spirituality for our day.[15] Dunblane evoked very similar themes, particularly in relation to the ages of the murdered children, whose perceived connection to the spiritual realm often seemed to be in inverse proportion to their corruption by the rationalizing forces which again had been responsible for their tragic end.

## The tactile and symbolic

Another prominent factor was the intuitive utilization of tactile and symbolic ways of accessing reality. This relates directly to the pilgrimage theme, for on a pilgrimage the various elements that are common to all the pilgrims (clothes, songs and so on) 'create a sacred atmosphere that intensifies sensitivity to the symbols that compose it'.[16] Symbols have the power to deal with a sense of experienced powerlessness: the very least they do is to give people a feeling that they know what they are doing, and are actually in control of a situation that otherwise seems chaotic. In life, people flocked to see Diana, taking her gifts, and expecting her to respond and change things (which she evidently did). Was the throwing of flowers at her coffin an expression of the same hope? The fundamental relationship between everyday spirituality, symbols and tactile experiences is one of the universal aspects of being human, and is a key way in which oral peoples have traditionally handled pain and discontinuity. One of the major ironies of our situation today is that Western culture is rapidly reverting to the characteristics of an oral culture which many thought had disappeared for good. Though we have high levels of literacy, increasing numbers, even of educated middle-class people, choose to adopt a lifestyle of functional illiteracy, and in this situation the adequacy of faith will be judged not on the basis of intellectual discourse, but by its

---

[15]  This is a good example of the recycling of existing traditions in popular spirituality, already discussed in the first three chapters of this book.

[16]  A. H. Mathias Zahniser, *Symbol and Ceremony* (Monrovia, CA: MARC, 1997), 141.

capacity to help people get through the night and then wake to new possibilities in the morning.[17] This way of being has largely disappeared from the horizons of Western Christianity, being either ignored altogether or dismissed as unchristian superstition. In consequence, we find it difficult, if not impossible, to forge meaningful connections between revealed aspects of faith and the use of mythical, ahistorical and archetypal images to connect with the meaning of life in the context of a wider cosmos.

## The power of stories

When analytical theological discourse fails because we are wrestling with questions to which there is no obvious answer, nor even an appropriate response in terms of the processes of reason and logic, stories are a key source of healing. In the mourning relating to both Dunblane and Diana, telling stories played a significant role in helping people to deal with the horror of what had happened. I was myself caught up in the aftermath of the Dunblane tragedy (which happened just a short drive from my home), and telling the story of people I met, things that took place, both in my church and in the wider community, became a way of coping. Others found that the events of those days evoked hidden memories of chance encounters with the children who died, with their parents – even with the gunman himself – and while these were often painful recollections, the sharing of them became a kind of corporate therapy. After Diana's death, people recalled how they, or someone they knew, had met her in unexpected situations, received a visit or a letter from her, or had been otherwise inspired by her example. Telling stories was a way to carry on, while also moving beyond mere survival into a celebration of the strength of the human spirit. In both cases, this ongoing telling of stories has taken on an almost sacramental flavour, undergirded by the need to remember, not allowing the memory to falter. The release of CDs, the wearing of ribbons, even the purchase of souvenirs, all fulfil this basic need. Moreover, this is a redemptive need, for by purchasing these items, or making

---

[17] For an especially thoughtful approach to sharing the gospel with such people, see Tex Sample, *Ministry in an Oral Culture* (Louisville, KY: Westminster/John Knox Press, 1994).

donations to trust funds, people with no stories of their own are able to identify themselves with the bigger story. It is easy to be cynical about some of this, but underlying it all is a genuine desire on the part of many people to see things change for the better. They want to have a stake in the bigger metanarrative – even when it focuses on suffering – because that opens up the possibility of redemption, not only for others, but frequently for themselves too.[18] It is a cliché to say that people can never be the same after tragedy strikes, but in these cases that is more true of more people than we sometimes imagine. The existing prior identification of Diana as in some sense a redemptive person herself merely highlighted the potentially redemptive nature of the grieving, something that will no doubt continue through pilgrimage to her grave and the Althorp estate where she spent her childhood.

### The grand vision

In the midst of all this – and contrary to all the predictions of post-modern theorists – there has undoubtedly surfaced a renewed search for some metanarrative that will put these fragments of human experience into a wider context. The human spirit has a constant need for value-communicating myths, and these events

---

[18] I had a striking personal example of that, when a story I had shared informally was seized upon by others to whom it spoke, and I found it being published in newspapers as far away as New Zealand, not to mention its unexpected appearance on dozens of sites on the World Wide Web. It was more than a year later that I eventually published it myself, in *Faith in a Changing Culture*, 28–30 – by which time it had been so thoroughly incorporated into the Dunblane mythology that some people expressed surprise to discover it was actually my story! Douglas Davies has proposed that people tell stories at such times as a way of endeavouring to gain spiritual merit for themselves, by sharing vicariously, as it were, in the good deeds of others – and as such, he dismisses it as contrary to the Christian understanding of grace. But this understanding does not address the nature of many of the stories told in the wake of the Hillsborough and Dunblane tragedies, which regularly focused on episodes that, had they been handled differently, might have avoided the tragedies altogether. Far from constituting a claim to 'cheap grace', the redemptive function of such stories was firmly rooted in confession and repentance. Cf. Douglas J. Davie, 'Popular Reaction to the Death of Princess Diana', *Expository Times* 109/6 (1997–98), 173–176.

have provided a particularly powerful one. In a culture struggling with the reality of post-Nazi humanism, which seemed to extinguish for ever the possibility that human endeavour could by itself get things right and embody the divine, the events following the Dunblane shootings and Diana's death have pushed some central archetypal buttons in people's corporate psyche.[19]

The relatively short space of time separating these two incidents ensured that many people made an intuitive link between them, seeing their own responses and reactions as in some way a journey 'From Dunblane to Diana,' which (to put a Christian spin on it) easily became a pilgrimage 'From the Massacre of the Innocents to the Crucifixion – and Beyond'. Over the last two decades, Hollywood movies have made us increasingly expectant of the intervention of external figures who will bring redemptive answers from beyond ourselves.[20] The Dunblane children were – and still are – regularly referred to as angels. Did Diana in death embody even more powerfully the elusive possibility that we (or someone like us) might yet break through and be both human and divine? In a site on the World Wide Web entitled *Forever Young*, the claim was made that 'Never in the history of the world has the death of one individual affected so many people . . .'[21] Whether or not the Christocentric overtones were intended, that seems to be the context in which much of the post-Diana rhetoric is most

---

[19] Though formulated in a completely different context, all the elements in Wayne C. Booth's proposal for five marks of a 'religion' leading to the emergence of a metanarrative were overtly present in the events post-Dunblane and Diana: (i) insistence that the world is flawed; (ii) insistence that the flaws be seen in the light of the Unflawed; (iii) people seeing themselves as in some sense part of the brokenness; (iv) awareness of a requirement for us to do something about it, to heal ourselves and others, that is somehow embodied in the nature of things; (v) acceptance of this cosmic requirement, even if it is unpleasant or personally painful. Cf. Wayne C. Booth, 'Deconstruction as a Religious Revival', in David A. Hoekema and Bobby Fung, *Christianity and Culture in the Crossfire* (Grand Rapids: Eerdmans, 1997), 131–154.

[20] For discussions of this and related phenomena, see Robert Short, *The Gospel from Outer Space* (London: Fount, 1983); Donald R. Mott and Cheryl McAllister Saunders, *Steven Spielberg* (London: Columbus Books, 1986), esp. 110–128; J. R. Lewis (ed), *The Gods have Landed: New Religions from Other Worlds* (Albany, NY: State University of New York Press, 1995).

[21] http://pages.prodigy.com/Diana/

readily located.[22] Consider the following correspondences between the story of Diana and the story of Christ:

- She came from humble and/or obscure origins, and her true significance was only appreciated when it was too late.

- She was an outsider in the world in which she operated.

- She was a person of special compassion, concerned for children, the meek and oppressed, the afflicted and the powerless – because she was one of them.

- She had access to special powers, based on different standards than most of us adopt in everyday life. She brought about 'miracles' of healing, lifting up those at the very edges of society (AIDS victims, lepers, people disfigured by land mines), and displayed unique gifts serving the cause of truth and justice, apparently able to harness the energies of the rich and powerful to causes that they would otherwise not have supported. She was a new kind of 'star child', capable of changing the unchangeable.

- She was opposed by the ideological power-brokers of the day – able to save others, but not ultimately able to save herself.

- She was hunted down by the agents of authority (paparazzi, et al.), in life and even to the point of death.

- She died a very public, very cruel, lingering death, which left her innate beauty disfigured and her body physically broken.

- She was laid to rest in a completely new grave site, never before used for that purpose.

---

[22] I began by imagining that Diana might be likened to the mythology surrounding the Virgin Mary, but I soon concluded that such apparent similarities are much less overt, and probably would never have suggested themselves as appropriate references apart from the fact that she was a woman. Popular portrayals show her not as the virgin, but as the Christ-figure.

Moreover, no implausible leaps of imagination are required to trace such correspondences, for all these and more were explicitly spelled out in Elton John's song 'Candle in the Wind', as also in the funeral oration delivered by Diana's brother, the Earl Spencer.[23] Most of them are, of course, a matter of perspective. For example, it is only relatively true that she was of humble origins (she was actually born into the English aristocracy), and while she was the victim of the media, she also courted their attention, and used them for her own purposes. But it is in this very ambivalence of her personality and lifestyle that she so obviously evokes Christ images – for example, in the way the New Testament represents Jesus of Nazareth as at once a humble nonentity (born in obscurity, working as a carpenter, and so on), while at the same time presenting him as a celestial being (descendant of the royal house of David and, indeed, Son of God and co-creator of the entire universe). There are also some things missing from this checklist. Because this is real life, and not the Hollywood special-effects department, there are – so far – no resurrection appearances, such as allegedly happened after the

---

[23] Some significant references in this regard would be the following:
(1) From 'Candle in the Wind'
   'may you ever grow in our hearts'
   'You were the grace that placed itself where lives were torn apart'
   'Now you belong to heaven and the stars spell out your name'
   '. . . your footsteps will always fall here, along England's greenest hills'
   'our nation's golden child'
   'who'll miss the wings of your compassion'
(2) From the funeral oration:
   'a symbol of selfless humanity . . . standard-bearer for the rights of the truly downtrodden . . . who transcended nationality'
   'your intuition . . . your instinctive feel for what was really important in all our lives . . . your God-given sensitivity'
   'her innermost feelings of suffering that made it possible for her to connect with her constituency of the rejected . . . childlike in her desire to do good . . . her vulnerability . . . her honesty'
   'genuinely good intentions sneered at by the media . . . a permanent quest . . . to bring her down . . . genuine goodness is threatening to those at the opposite end of the moral spectrum'
   'the most hunted person of the modern age'
   'steering these two exceptional young men so that their souls are not simply immersed by duty and tradition but can sing openly as you planned'

death of Elvis Presley in 1977.[24] But there has been the 1990s equivalent, namely the emergence of a 'Church of Princess Diana', based on channelled messages from Diana's spirit, and giving advice and guidance on matters pertaining to life in the new millennium, all of it contained in a 'Bible' according to Diana. The recipient of this information is someone calling himself Chairman Yao, a native of Tibet, who claims to have had many previous lives, and who describes himself as 'the Ascended Master who will usher us into the New Age'.[25]

To find such sentiments, however, one does not have to look so far afield. As they make their way round the tourist trail on the Althorp Estate, Diana's childhood home in rural Northamptonshire and now her burial site, visitors pass through a neoclassical temple that has become, in effect, a shrine to her memory. Overlooking the lake and her grave, this contains a cameo portrait of the princess and, on a matching tablet, the inscription 'Whenever you are in need, call for me and I will answer'. The phrase is actually taken from one of her speeches, but in the total context in which it is displayed there can scarcely be any doubt that those who placed it there must have been well aware of the implicit association it makes with Diana as an angelic, if not divine being available both to hear and to answer prayers. The World Wide Web has literally thousands of sites dedicated to Diana, including at least one which offers the opportunity to pray to and for her, by providing a menu from which visitors can select Buddhist, Christian, Hindu, Islamic, Jewish, New Age, Sikh or Wiccan prayers, depending on their spiritual preference.[26]

It is easy to dismiss all this somewhat cynically. But there are some serious concerns here, and it is important for Christians not to throw out the baby of true spiritual search along with the bathwater of media hype and New Age froth. From the point of view of Christian witness, we need to consider the clear connection between these themes and the Christ figure of the New Testament. To what extent does John 1:11–12 provide a fitting epitaph for

---

[24]  On the development of the Elvis mythology, see Christine King, 'His Truth Goes Marching On', in Reader and Walter, *Pilgrimage in Popular Culture*, 92–104.

[25]  See the web site http://www.dianaspeaks.org/

[26]  http://www.royalnetwork.com/hearts

Diana? 'She came to the world that was her own, but her own people did not accept her. Yet to all who did accept and believe, she gave the right to become children of God.' What does that mean in terms of the church's mission? Much more work needs to be done before an answer to that can adequately be teased out.[27] This is not the place to pursue it further, except to note that, missiologically speaking, the similarities between these two great archetypal stories is something that the church cannot afford to ignore.

## Understanding the Cultural Context

It is not at all difficult to make a superficial link between all this and the much-discussed paradigm shift from modernity to post-modernity, but determining the exact relationship between these trends is more complex than merely putting a label on it all. In particular, it does make a difference whether the Diana phenomenon was a unique experience, unlikely to be repeated, or whether it is the latest episode in a significant nascent form of popular spiritual expression. I wish to suggest that it is the latter. Without (I hope) being pretentious about it, I would argue that the mourning for Diana was an entirely predictable outcome of the trends that I had myself noted in my book *Faith in a Changing Culture*, published only four months before her death. In spite of that, I was still taken by surprise when it all happened, for two reasons. First, one rarely gets such outstanding empirical support for one's theories about spirituality and mission so soon after putting them forward. And second, I had accepted the conclusions of those sociologists who had argued that historical antecedents such as the Anfield pilgrimage

---

[27] One of the things that happened with Diana was that a vein of pain was opened up and tapped into, invoking archetypal images that related to existing grief, past loss, and so on, and this was only heightened because Diana was like us, but not like us – in theological terms, perhaps both 'human' and 'divine', though not sinless. Both in life and death, she evoked what Victor Turner called 'instrumental symbols' (i.e. symbols with significance in particular situations), and the challenge for the church will be to discern how these can be employed to highlight the 'dominant symbols' of the Christian tradition (i.e. values or beliefs that are held to be universally true). Cf. Victor Turner, *The Forest of Symbols* (Ithaca, NY: Cornell University Press, 1967).

(when tens of thousands turned the home stadium of Liverpool Football Club into a shrine following the Hillsborough football stadium disaster) were a localized phenomenon entirely contingent on the culture of Merseyside, which everyone recognizes is distinctive even within the UK.[28] The events in Dunblane ought to have alerted me to the fact that this was part of a pattern of massive cultural change, though once again there were what looked like special local factors, particularly the Scottish dimension and the kind of close-knit community that was involved. However, I believe we can now trace a clear trend linking all the recent examples of public grief, but especially Anfield – Dunblane – Diana, and see them as symptomatic of the shift from modernity to post-modernity. As such, they are of interest not only to cultural analysts, but also – and especially – to the churches in relation to their missionary task.

Furthermore, they help to locate what post-modernity might mean in relation to the church's mission. In particular, they give support for the opinion that people are, for the most part, 'post-modern' in a sociological sense rather than ideologically 'postmodern' in terms of their worldview. The way in which people handled Diana's death – particularly the underlying implied search for new self-created metanarratives – supports the opinion that the end of our cultural love affair with modernity has come about more on pragmatic grounds than as a result of philosophical principle. The search for new ways of being is driven by forces that are 'post-modern' (where the hyphen indicates something emerging 'after' the 'modern' ways of doing things have outlived their usefulness), rather than by the nostrums of 'postmodernism' in the ideological sense.[29] Popular culture (as distinct, perhaps, from

---

[28] Cf. A. Walter, 'The Mourning after Hillsborough', *Sociological Review* 39/3 (1991), 599–625; Grace Davie, 'You'll Never Walk Alone: The Anfield pilgrim-age', in Reader and Walter, *Pilgrimage in Popular Culture*, 201–219. In a personal communication (March 1998), Grace Davie commented: 'I was quite clearly wrong – what I thought was an exception turned out to be a prototype! I would never have dared to argue this in 1990.'

[29] David Lyon makes this distinction, though using the terms 'postmodernism' and 'postmodernity', with the first referring to the philosophical systems of think-ers such as Foucault, Derrida et al., and the latter being essentially a sociological reference to the collapse of the social, economic and political systems that typified

academic or intellectual culture) has not adopted some grand philosophical vision, but is simply aware of the deficiencies of inherited ways of doing things, foremost among which is a sense that the Enlightenment worldview has led to an unhealthy dismissal of the relevance of anything spiritual, and that the church – far from being the solution – is actually part of the problem. This in turn sheds further light on how the church has ended up in such serious decline while the culture is far more openly religious or spiritual than it has been for some considerable time. Could it be that, by its uncritical embracing of the culture of modernity, not only did the church historically accept some notions that were actually Christian heresies, but it also embraced the methods of modernity to such an extent that, at least in the West, Christians are actually incapable of imagining how to contextualize the gospel in a different cultural frame of reference? Is the church's predicament less a crisis of religion or spirituality, and more a crisis of culture, stemming from the fact that at a time when fewer and fewer people still find meaning within the culture of modernity, that is the only frame of reference in which the church knows how to operate?

## Challenges for the Churches

Related to this cultural challenge, we can also trace several specific issues that have been highlighted by recent events. This is not an exhaustive list, nor is it possible to do any more than summarize them briefly.

### The creation of a 'non-religious' image for the church

At a time when politics is increasingly regarded as a power struggle among diverse interest groups, the churches are easily perceived as just one pressure group among the many that clamour for our attention. Ironically, this seems to have been encouraged by the churches' own self-conscious engagement with social and political issues, which was undertaken for perfectly good and justifiable

---

[29] (continued) the 'modernity' of the Enlightenment. As he points out, the two cannot be entirely separated, but it still remains a useful distinction. See David Lyon, *Postmodernity* (Buckingham: Open University Press, 1994).

reasons, both theological and strategic. Though this was the last thing that was ever intended, the resultant image can be one of a church which is 'unspiritual' in the sense that it is more interested in the material than in the religious – and for that reason, no more (or less) deserving of being taken seriously than any other special interest group in society.[30] Encouraging this perception is the ready acceptance of an 'establishment' image, which inevitably means that when commitment to other institutions with their base in modernity diminishes, the church is bound to feel the impact.[31] I would be the last to argue for a separation of mission and social action – indeed, I see them as two sides of the same coin, and would argue that a truly Christian spirituality ought to hold them together in creative tension – but for that very reason we need to work at ensuring that we develop a holistic understanding of faith, in which the spiritual is no less central than the material.[32]

## Perpetuation of an over-cognitive culture

The extent to which this is the case varies from one Christian tradition to another, though it is generally true that, to cope with

---

[30]  It is significant in this context to note that two observers of the American scene – from very different parts of the theological spectrum – have related the decline of the American churches, first of the mainline denominations and more recently of the religious Right – to their concern for political issues at the expense of specifically spiritual values. The moral and social issues with which the British churches have concerned themselves are mostly different from those in the USA, but this understanding of the predicament of Christians in a post-modern culture is not as irrelevant as it seems, and will repay further reflection. See Tony Campolo, *Can Mainline Denominations Make a Comeback?* (Valley Forge, PA: Judson Press, 1995); Robert Wuthnow, *The Crisis in the Churches: Spiritual Malaise, Fiscal Woe* (New York: OUP, 1997).

[31]  The church's problems of falling commitment and membership are common to other institutions from the era of modernity, such as trades unions and political parties, which are also in serious, if not terminal decline.

[32]  Martin Luther King Jr must have been one of the most outstanding examples of how to hold together in creative tension these two polarities, constantly insisting that his political activism was a natural outcome of his primary calling as a preacher of the gospel. Of course, his understanding of 'preaching' was born of a different social reality than the conventional definitions of British Christians! Cf. Richard Lischer, *The Preacher King* (New York: OUP, 1995).

church, people need to be able to make sense of things through processing abstract concepts, and those who more naturally deal with problems in an intuitive, artistic or creative way will find little that speaks to them. On the whole, today's Christians tend to prefer the propositional, and express varying degrees of uneasiness with image, symbols and, particularly, the imagination. This is true even of those traditions which historically have been most firmly rooted in a more visual and interactive spirituality. We need a renewed theology of the human person and of spiritual growth.

### Embarrassment with the mystical, the numinous, and the spiritual

Western Christians have not only bought into a cognitive culture, but one that is dominated by rationalism and materialism. There is significant embarrassment about such things as angels, heaven, the after-life, and so on. At best, the church seems to speak uncomfortably of them – at worst, it gives the impression that it no longer believes in such things. All this makes us look oddly out of tune with a world that sometimes seems interested in nothing else.[33] One of the greatest ironies of the twentieth century is the way that in the 1920s and 1930s, Protestant theologians were falling over themselves to 'demythologize' the gospel, at exactly the moment that Albert Einstein was inaugurating the move towards a 'remythologized' scientific paradigm.[34] We are still struggling with the consequences of that.

### Issues of control, power and patriarchy

To a greater degree than most of us would like to acknowledge, the inherited organizational and theological styles of all our churches find their roots in the patriarchal culture of the British Empire (and,

---

[33] A survey carried out by NOP Solutions for the TV satellite Sci-Fi Channel in April 1998 discovered that three out of four British people believe there is life elsewhere in the universe, an impression that can be readily confirmed by a visit to the 'Body, Mind and Spirit' section of any major bookstore, where books on angels and extraterrestrial beings are top sellers.

[34] This mythologized science has of course now become a major impetus in the search for new spiritualities in the Western world: cf. among many others Fritjof Capra, *The Web of Life* (London: HarperCollins, 1996).

beyond that, in Christendom and ancient Rome). Not only has this led to many people feeling marginalized by the churches, but it has also nurtured an unhealthy domination of Christian thinking by an essentially heretical view of God, deriving from Greek philosophy, in which all our theological outcomes need to be 'successful', and where there is little or no space for tragedy and suffering, or for emotions like grief and failure. Alongside this is a deep-seated unwillingness to allow – still less empower – those who are not the 'right' people, to construct their own do-it-yourself theology and spirituality. This is a major issue, for central to all the events mentioned here has been a form of spirituality and worship that grows from the grass roots up, rather than being imposed from the top down.[35] Theologians and church leaders are happy enough to articulate the need for a servant church, but it requires more than fine words. To put it into practice would mean we ought to be providing the infrastructure of spirituality, not its superstructure. How and what to build on that infrastructure will then be the responsibility of the individual, and facing that responsibility is a key component of what gives life its spiritual meaning.

I am aware of having stated the issues somewhat starkly here: it would certainly be appropriate to debate the various nuances of what I am claiming. But the key missiological issue is not so much whether all this is true in the absolute sense, but whether it approximates to people's perceptions of the church – and on the whole I believe it does.

## Revisiting the Key Themes

This is not the place for an exhaustive exposition of how Christians might engage creatively with the renewed popular spirituality of our

---

[35] Though some liturgical purists have complained that Diana's funeral liturgy bore no resemblance to any rite legally approved for use in the Church of England, in practical terms few would disagree that the authorities of Westminster Abbey did, by any standards, a great job in the crafting of a funeral service that would be appropriate to the occasion. Even so, one of the most significant moments of all was when applause generated outside in the streets invaded the top-down spirituality of what was going on inside the Abbey.

day.[36] Still, it will be worth drawing attention to the fact that there are significant spiritual riches within the Christian tradition at precisely those points that I have argued were central to what took place post-Dunblane and in the wake of Diana's death.

## Pilgrimage

The role of pilgrimage in the Bible is obvious, and fairly central. It occurs everywhere as a key image for the understanding of faith, whether in relation to the literal visiting of places, or in historical episodes such as the Passover and Exodus traditions, or the symbolic re-enactment of such historical moments in the worship of the Jerusalem temple. In addition, the language of pilgrimage is frequently used in a metaphorical way to refer to faith as a journey. Protestants in particular have generally felt happier with the individualistic and internalized understanding of pilgrimage classically represented in Bunyan's *Pilgrim's Progress* than with the tangible, experiential, moving pilgrimage reflected in the models of worship presented in the Bible and continued in the original architectural intent of many ancient church buildings, with their open spaces within which processionals and other forms of movement were a good deal easier to orchestrate than they would be in today's churches, with their clutter of furniture. Does the church have something to relearn and rediscover here? We should not underestimate the extent to which this may be threatening for some, as pilgrimage also embodies an understanding of faith itself as something dynamic, growing, provisional and evolving – a big difference from the patterns of faith inherited from modernity, where everything had to be rationalized, predictable, commodified and neatly definable.

## Spontaneity

For similar reasons, the church is often afraid of spontaneity, of allowing people to create their own spiritual spaces and formulate

---

[36] For further discussion of that, see my *Faith in a Changing Culture*; Philip Johnson, 'Postmodernity, New Age, and Christian Mission', *in Lutheran Theological Journal* 31/3 (1997), 115–124; and my forthcoming book *The McDonaldization of the Church* (London: Darton Longman & Todd, 2000).

their own expressions of faith. Who knows what might happen when the 'wrong' sort of people get their hands on matters that hitherto have been the preserve of those with the 'right' sort of training, and the approval and authorization of the regular institutional structures? The question is easily answered, of course, for that is precisely what has happened among many groups of non-Western Christians, often under the leadership of women and children, not to mention the downtrodden and oppressed – and the result has been massive growth of the church to a point where, in world terms, white Western Christians are now outnumbered by others two to one. At a time when British churches face serious decline, it is foolish to imagine that we have nothing to learn from this, though it cannot be denied that any learning might have to be at the expense of some of our most cherished notions. In spontaneous spirituality, creeds are likely to be less important than autobiography and the shared search for meaning, and the rediscovery of praxis as a key expression of faith will challenge the inherited supremacy of rationality over experience.

### The tactile and symbolic

Perhaps nothing goes so directly to the heart of much of our present predicament. Theologically, there is a challenge here to our apparent inability – or unwillingness – to engage with the question of formulating a creation-centred spirituality which will be able to embrace both the historical Jesus and the cosmic Christ or, to express it differently, the relationship between the cognitive and the affective. Ironically, there is no shortage of material for bridging this gap within the Christian tradition, for while the (cognitive) understanding of the Bible has always been central for theologians, for most Christians throughout most of history, regular devotion has needed to focus on other forms of spirituality, for the simple reason that they have been illiterate people. Mosaics, painting, stained glass, statues, carvings, music and other artistic and symbolic expressions of meaning were natural components of a holistic spirituality that engaged with all the senses of smell, touch, vision, hearing and so on. Just as the divine Word became flesh through the incarnation, so the Bible and its message was incarnated and made accessible to the wider population through the use of relevant images, most of which were both tactile and symbolic. The use of literature was originally related to such cultural concerns, as exemplified by the first generation of the church, and later the Reformers who, when they found themselves in a situation where the printed book was emerging as a medium of mass-communication, naturally contextualized the gospel within that culture. Unfortunately, subsequent generations have not been so perceptive, and even today some Christians do not appreciate that the traditional book-based era is coming to an end. Under the mistaken belief that the only way to preserve the integrity of the divine word must be through a cognitive, propositional, book-centred understanding of faith, Christians have effectively left the new visual and tactile image-making machine of post-modern culture to search for its own values with which to portray and understand the human condition. In the process, the Word has not become flesh, but has been reimprisoned in words – something that is not only bad communication strategy, but bad theology as well, for it is in effect a heretical denial of the incarnation. The notion that only things with a cognitive and rational base can be meaningful is not true either to human nature or to the gospel. Oral cultures have always had a holistic foundation, endowing all of life with spiritual meaning – and usually making that connection through the use of symbols and ritual. In the post-modern context (which has more similarities with oral cultures than most observers will admit), these are the things that will deepen faith and bring life into harmony with belief. These are also the very things that Western theism has generally devalued, but which will need to be rediscovered if there is to be an effective Christian witness in the new context.[37] In a recent book Clark Pinnock – whose own pilgrimage from neo-fundamentalism to a highly eclectic, but firmly Christian, spirituality is itself an illuminating example of what will be involved for some in the move from a modernist to post-modern way of being church – concludes: 'We do ourselves harm when we eliminate arts,

---

[37] Paul Hiebert has identified three levels of problem-solving in traditional societies: (i) high religion, based on cosmic beings or forces; (ii) folk or low religion, magic and astrology; and (iii) folk social and natural science. He argues that Western Christianity has operated on the high level (i), and the lowest level (iii), albeit replacing folk science with Western science – but has excluded altogether the middle layer, which is where faith is put to work and related to everyday concerns such as work and health, through symbols and ceremonies. See his 'The Flaw of the Excluded Middle', in *Missiology* 10/1 (1982), 35–47; *Anthropological Insights for Missionaries* (Grand Rapids: Baker, 1985).

drama, color, vestments, pageantry, incense, saints, calendars, lectionary, sculpture'.[38]

## The power of stories

In his book *Generation X*, based on the imaginary conversations of three friends who opt out of the mainstream to live in the Arizona desert, Douglas Coupland observes that 'it's not healthy to live life as a succession of isolated little cool moments. Either our lives become stories, or there's just no way to get through them . . . this is why the three of us left our lives behind us and came to the desert – to tell stories and to make our own lives worthwhile tales in the process.' Later on, he admits that 'most of us have only two or three genuinely interesting moments in our lives, the rest is filler . . . at the end of our lives most of us will be lucky if any of those moments connect together to form a story that anyone would find remotely interesting'.[39]

Even Hollywood has called the Bible *The Greatest Story Ever Told* and, like the stories that unfolded around the tragedies of Dunblane and Diana, it is a story with a redemptive purpose. Telling the stories of faith, relating them to our own personal stories, discovering new images of Christ that will speak with power to today's generation, may lead to a more open-ended sharing of faith than some Christians will be happy with. But the very fact that stories leave spaces for meanings, and create new possibilities for the exploration of spirituality, means that they will more effectively address the concerns of everyday life, cross cultural boundaries, and invite the active participation and commitment of those who share in their telling.

## The grand vision

Douglas Coupland, to whom I have just referred, is one of the most perceptive observers of the spirituality of our age. In his book *Life*

---

[38] C. H. Pinnock, *Flame of Love: A Theology of the Holy Spirit* (Downers Grove, IL: InterVarsity Press, 1996), 122.

[39] Douglas Coupland, *Generation X* (New York: St Martins Press, 1991), quotations from pp. 8 and 23–24.

*After God*, at the end of three hundred pages of stories expressing the plight of what he calls 'the first generation raised without religion', he finds himself in the quietness of a temperate rainforest in his native British Columbia, about to plunge into a cool stream of water where he hopes to find a fresh angle on life and its meaning. 'Now – here is my secret,' he writes. 'I tell it to you with an openness of heart that I doubt I shall ever achieve again, so I pray that you are in a quiet room as you hear these words. My secret is that I need God – that I am sick and can no longer make it alone. I need God to help me give, because I no longer seem capable of giving; to help me be kind, as I no longer seem capable of kindness; to help me love, as I seem beyond being able to love.'[40] At a time when many others are openly echoing his words, the church often seems to be enmeshed in its own trivialities, and to those outside presents itself as having lost its own grand vision – the foundational biblical vision of a world in which God is at work, together with the apostolic vision of how the innate spiritual search of humanity can be a pointer towards the gospel. The events of recent years have provided several such signs. What we need now are Christians with the vision, the spirituality, the humanity and the compassion to know how to utilize them effectively.

---

[40] Douglas Coupland, *Life After God* (New York: Simon & Schuster, 1994), 359.

# Chapter 6

# Cultural Change, Church Life and the Future Shape of Christian Ministry[1]

## Introduction

'The times they are a'changing . . .' So sang Bob Dylan back in the 1960s, expressing ideas that at the time seemed alien and unlikely to many people – but which, with the benefit of hindsight, we can see to have been a prophetic perception of what was taking place. It is not only that our culture has changed: it continues to do so, and at a very fast speed. Things now change so quickly that, by the time we have found the solution to today's problems, the questions themselves have altered – and governments and businesses, as well as ordinary people, are struggling to keep pace with it all.

As we have seen already, different people have their own favourite labels to describe what is happening. Management consultants might say that we have moved from the Machine Age to the Systems Age; New Age activists might say we are at the close of the Age of Pisces, and the dawn of the Age of Aquarius. Others prefer to speak of the collapse of modernity, and the emergence of the post-modern world. Whatever the preferred terminology – and they are all referring to what is essentially the same phenomenon – there is a clear consensus that the old ways of doing things which have dominated Western thinking for the last five hundred years or more have run their course, and if there is to be a future for humankind in the next millennium, we must work out new ways of living.

---

[1] A revised version of a paper previously circulated as *Cultural Change and the Future Shape of Christian Ministry* (London: Christian Research Association, 1997), CRA Leader's Briefing No. 6.

Many sensitive people look back on some of the great events of previous generations, and regret the way in which Western values were forcibly imposed on the inhabitants of other lands, and wonder if the negative aspects of imperial expansion have not outweighed whatever positive benefits there may have been.

But the imposition of its own values on the rest of the world is just one tiny part of what Western culture – the culture of modernity – has come to represent. It is a symbol, if you like, that can be applied in many other areas of Western achievement. So in science and technology, for instance, few people would wish to turn the clock back to a time before the invention of modern methods of transportation – yet in the process of moving ourselves around with ever greater efficiency, we all now know that we are gradually destroying the ozone layer and causing untold damage to the environment in the process. Or in medicine, no one would regret the discovery of antibiotics and anaesthetics – yet increasing numbers of people feel dissatisfied with what they perceive as a mechanistic and dehumanizing form of healthcare, which can keep bodies ticking over in much the same way as a technician can adjust the engine of a car, but often seems incapable of addressing more profound issues of human well-being related to the mind and the spirit.

Our culture is trapped in a love–hate relationship with its heritage – not wishing to reverse the process of history, but certainly all too conscious of the negative aspects of what we have inherited from the past. As a consequence, there is a strongly felt and clearly articulated demand for quite fundamental change. Moreover, there is a growing conviction that this is not going to be just a matter of fiddling around the edges and remodelling a few things: what is now required is a completely different way of understanding the cosmos itself, and our place in it as human beings. Albert Einstein, whose articulation of the theory of relativity played a major part in undermining traditional Enlightenment science, is credited with having once commented that 'No problem can be solved from the same consciousness that created it. We must learn to see the world anew.' This search for a new way of seeing the world is at the heart of the cultural change which is now taking place. The entire frame of reference within which our forebears understood things has been discarded, and what is emerging is not just a revised version of the *status quo*, but a completely new way of understanding the world: a paradigm shift at least as significant as that which happened when Galileo discovered that the world was not flat, or when Newton and others came up with the notion (now discredited) of 'laws of nature'. Reference has been made in previous chapters to the optimism with which certain sections of the New Age believe they are in the process of actually recreating the world itself. More prosaically, Alvin Toffler has observed that 'A new civilization is emerging in our lives . . . This new civilization brings with it new family styles; changed ways of working, loving, and living . . . Millions are already attuning their lives to the rhythms of tomorrow . . . The dawn of this new civilization is the single most explosive fact of our lifetimes.'[2]

## Setting the Context

A traditional Chinese proverb advises, 'Whoever does not know the village they have come from will never find the village they are looking for.' We will not find our true Christian calling in the new world order without first understanding our heritage from the past. Such exploration could begin in any number of places. But René Descartes (1595–1650) is as good a starting point as any, with his Latin dictum *Cogito ergo sum* (I am thinking, therefore I am).[3] As a result of the pervasive influence of this notion, personhood has been defined in relation to what people think and the processes of rationality and argument, rather than with reference to other human values and capacities. The idea itself, of course, ultimately goes back well beyond Descartes: it can be found in Greek philosophical thinking in an even more radical form, which denigrated the whole of physical existence in favour of the 'reason' that was supposed to be at the centre of all things. Within that cultural stream, thinking was often set in opposition to feeling and, as a consequence, the marginalization of feelings has been a key characteristic of Western

---

[2] Alvin Toffler, *The Third Wave* (New York: Bantam, 1980), 9.
[3] R. Descartes, 'Discourse on the Method', part 4, section 32, in J. Cottingham, R. Stoothoff, D. Murdoch (eds), *Philosophical Writings of Descartes* (Cambridge: CUP, 1985), vol. 1, 127.

culture (including Christian culture) to such an extent that many Western people, men in particular, simply have no life skills with which to handle emotions and feelings, or to relate to the numinous, the mystical and the spiritual.

With the final collapse of all the empires, and the realization of the damage we have done to the environment, our culture has now woken up to the impoverishment of spirit that has been induced by reliance on just this one way of seeing the world. Three things have made a particular contribution to this change, and have a special relevance for church life and witness in the new situation.

### Brain science

Put simply, modern brain science has shown that to be Western in this traditional Cartesian sense is literally to be half-witted, because it values and uses only one half of the human brain.[4] Western culture has been dominated and directed by those skills that are located in the left hemisphere of the brain – skills of analysis, of logic, of abstract thinking, of speech and of grammar. But we cannot be whole persons unless we learn to use all our brains, and that means valuing the different kinds of skill that are controlled by the right side of the brain: imagination, feeling, metaphor, colour, texture and so on. Psychology professor Marilyn Ferguson highlights this as one of the major problems with the philosophy that has traditionally inspired Western healthcare when she comments that 'Warmth, intuition, and imagination are precisely the characteristics likely to be screened out by the emphasis on scholastic standing and test scores. The right brain, in effect, was being denied access to medical school. There were no quotas for creativity.'[5]

---

[4] The pioneer in this field was Roger Sperry, who won the 1981 Nobel Prize in Physiology and Medicine for his research. Cf. his early paper 'Brain Bisection and Consciousness', in J. Eccles (ed.), *Brain and Conscious Experience* (New York: Springer-Verlag, 1966). For an accessible survey of subsequent research, see Sally P. Springer and Gertz Deitsch, *Left Brain, Right Brain* (New York: Freeman, 4th edn, 1993). A practical application of these insights would be Tony Buzan's *The Mind Map Book* (London: BBC, 1993) or, for a distinctively Christian application, see Walter Wink, *Transforming Bible Study* (London: Mowbray, 2nd edn, 1990).
[5] Marilyn Ferguson, *The Aquarian Conspiracy* (London: Paladin, 1982), 293.

## The global village

At the beginning of the twentieth century it was still possible to imagine that being Western and accepting Western values and lifestyles, was the only way to live the good life. Greater awareness of other cultures and faiths has made it obvious that things are not so simple. Empirically, the majority of the world's people in all times and places have lived their lives according to quite different principles. The following list highlights some of the major contrasts:[6]

| Scientific Worldview | Poetic Worldview |
| --- | --- |
| Precise | Imprecise |
| Reason/intellect | Emotions/intuition |
| Permanent | Provisional |
| Physical | Spiritual |
| Absolute | Ambiguous |
| Science/technology | Values |
| Propositional | Approximate |
| Western culture | Ethnic worldviews |
| Rational | Intuitive |
| Men | Women |
| Literal | Symbolic |
| Church | Spiritual quest |
| Worship | Personal needs |

To a large extent, the two columns can be identified with the qualities of 'left-brain thinking' (= the 'scientific worldview') and 'right-brain thinking' (= the 'poetic worldview'). Though there is a good deal of debate about the precise difference between Hebrew (= biblical) thinking and Greek (= secular) thinking, it would not be too misleading in addition to identify the scientific column with the Greeks and the poetic column with the

---

[6] For a discussion of the validity of this kind of typological characterization of 'Eastern' vs. 'Western' worldviews and attitudes, see Colin Campbell, 'The Easternisation of the West', in Bryan Wilson and Jamie Cresswell (eds), *New Religious Movements: Challenge and Response* (London: Routledge, 1999), 34–48.

Hebrews, at least if we use those terms in a typological sense.[7] The various headings then identify not only the philosophical notions underlying these distinctions, but also some of their practical repercussions. The diagram itself will repay further reflection, but there is no question that the development of Western Christianity has been almost wholly dominated by the values and concerns of what is here labelled 'scientific'.

Moreover, contrasts of this kind can also be expressed in other, more overtly spiritual ways. With increasing awareness of Eastern philosophy and religion, the notion of forces of yin and yang and the need for balance between them in order to achieve true wholeness in life has entered the vocabulary and thought world of increasing numbers of people, Christians included. If we forget for a moment the metaphysical origins of these concepts, and reflect on them as a typological understanding of two opposed ways of being, we can identify a series of contrasts like this:

| *Yang* | *Yin* |
| --- | --- |
| Masculine | Feminine |
| Demanding | Contractive |
| Aggressive | Responsive |
| Competitive | Co-operative |
| Rational | Intuitive |
| Analytic | Synthesizing |

It hardly needs any further comment for the similarities between the two diagrams to become immediately apparent, nor for the repercussions of this for Christian faith to be obvious. In each case, the column on the left represents those characteristics that

---

[7] I am aware of the possible distortions that can arise in using this terminology, not only historically, in the sense that Greek and Hebraic culture were much more closely interrelated in the days of the Roman empire than some previous scholars have allowed, but also in relation to some of the specific aspects of Herrew and Greek culture. So, for example, ancient Greek culture had a significant place for the arts, a feature which one might suppose would put it in the 'poetic' column, whereas Hebrew culture eschewed visual art (though not the dramatic arts). What this suggests is that the differences are not universally compartmentalized, which is why I emphasize that this is a 'typological' differentiation, rather than implying any historical or sociological categorization.

arguably have created most of the tensions in the world today, not only the tensions between people but also that most crucial tension of all, between people and the environment.[8] The column on the right, by contrast, highlights a different way of living and relating, which looks to be gentler and more relevant to life in the new millennium, and ultimately more redemptive in terms of healing the wounds of the world and its people. The question is: has the church become trapped in the wrong place?

### Science at the frontiers

When I was a student in the late 1960s, it was commonly supposed that science dealt with facts, whereas religion was only about opinions. That perception led many of my contemporaries to atheism, though even then cutting-edge science had already dealt the death-blow to such an understanding. Today, by contrast, it is taken for granted that science does not have the answers – indeed, that as traditionally practised in its Newtonian and Baconian forms, it scarcely knew the right questions. By 1994 in a throwaway aside that he felt no need to justify because he was confident no one would fundamentally challenge it, management professor Charles Handy could write of 'the myth of science, the idea that everything, in theory, could be understood, predicted and, therefore managed'.[9] Science no longer claims to tell us how things really are in some objective sense, certainly not within the context of a closed-system view of the universe. The whole agenda is now wide open. Following the groundbreaking work of Einstein, Heisenberg, Gödel, Mandelbrot and, more recently, Stephen Hawking, literally anything seems to be possible. As we have already observed in earlier chapters, some of the leading spiritual commentators of our day are also scientists – people like biologist Rupert Sheldrake and physicist Fritjof Capra, or psychologist Barry McWaters, who explains his own search for new light on the

---

[8] As with the previous contrast drawn between 'scientific' and 'poetic' worldviews, this is also a typological description. Though *yin* and *yang* respectively represent the feminine and the masculine, it is obviously not the case that all men display *yang* characteristics, nor all women the *yin*. But as a categorization, these are still useful distinctions.

[9] Charles Handy, *The Empty Raincoat* (London: Hutchinson, 1994), 17.

human condition in the following terms: 'We are listening for messages of guidance from every possible source; tuning in our astro-radios, talking to dolphins, and listening more and more attentively to the words of those among us with psychic abilities. Is there help out there? Is there guidance in here? Will anyone respond?'[10] Even Stephen Hawking, arguably the greatest scientist of our day, writing in the foreword to Lawrence Krauss's book *The Physics of Star Trek*, has commented that 'To confine our attention to terrestrial matters would be to limit the human spirit', and in the process he tacitly goes on to endorse the possibility of time travel.[11]

We have already explored the paradigm shift that is now taking place from several different perspectives. A particular concern for Christians ought to be the implication that the church is part of the problem that has brought our culture to this impasse, and for that reason cannot expect to be considered seriously as a possible solution to today's crisis. This focuses especially on the area of spirituality. In the 1980s, people were inclined to dismiss the church as dull, boring, old-fashioned or irrelevant, but today an increasing chorus is insisting that the church is 'unspiritual'. It is not always easy to define what people mean by 'spirituality' in this context, though it must be obvious that we will not make much progress by semantic hair-splitting about that. If those who are looking for spiritual answers do not find that the church speaks to them in a relevant and meaningful way, then Christians face a major problem of credibility and integrity and need to wake up and do something about it. It is no good blaming other people as if their questions are the problem: if they are their questions, and they are concerned with God and ultimate meaning in life, then the church's missionary mandate requires that we engage with them, and not reject them out of hand. They might prove to be awkward questions, but therein lies the problem: Christians too often like to give simple answers to questions that they have formulated themselves, because they think they know the answers to them.

Previous chapters have explored in some detail the nature of the spiritual search that is going on today. Let me here summarize

---

[10] Barry McWaters, *Conscious Evolution* (Los Angeles: New Age Press, 1981), 111–112.

[11] Lawrence M. Krauss, *The Physics of Star Trek* (London: HarperCollins, 1996), xi–xiii.

where all this has taken us. Three ages, or stages of development, may be discerned in Western culture. First was the period of the *pre-modern*, which in fact was most of history – a time dominated by 'superstition', 'mythology', and other pre-critical ways of understanding things. Then, with the Renaissance, the development of modern science, and the Enlightenment, came the period of *modernity*, with its commitment to the critical application of reason as the way to get things right, and a corresponding devaluing and demythologizing of what were perceived to be 'primitive' magical and religious worldviews. We now seem to be somewhere in the transition from modernity in that classical sense to whatever may follow it, conventionally labelled post-modernism though, as we have repeatedly observed, there is a good deal of uncertainty as to what exactly that means. Some things, though, are clear: the cultural climate in which we now find ourselves is increasingly post-critical, in the sense that it is questioning – indeed, rejecting – categories of reason and rationality. It is giving a much greater place to intuition, and is rapidly remythologizing our understanding of the world, not only through the spiritual search as defined by religious categories, but also in the discourse of modern science. In one sense, this is just a different way of expressing the same thing as the two diagrams used previously.

## Church and Culture

In this context, the church faces particular problems, both from beyond its own boundaries, and also from within. It is a matter of historical fact that the church was one of the major players in the European culture from which the worldview of modernity emerged. The precise nuances of the relationship between church, Christendom, Enlightenment, Renaissance and Reformation are highly complex, but they are sufficiently well established at least in broad outline for it to be impossible to deny the existence of close links. It seems indisputable that the development of Western individualism (something Christians in particular have come to regret) has an intrinsic connection with the Reformation emphasis on each individual being solely responsible for themselves before God. It is likewise undeniable that Western imperialism was a

logical development from the self-understanding of Christendom –
and that all these things had their philosophical roots in ancient
Greek (especially Aristotelian) thinking, which was mediated to the
West not in a 'pure' form, but through categories developed by
centuries of Christian theology. Technology, for its part, had
obvious roots in ancient Roman lifestyles, as applied and extended
within Christendom. In the light of all this, it is not difficult for
people to blame Christianity for most of the world's present ills,
especially in relation to the environment. Whether or not all this is
literally true, it is sufficiently true for enough people to think it is,
and inevitably, therefore, this perception is having a major impact
on the church's image in the world – as well as its mission – at the
present time.

In addition, however, the church faces a different, though
related, set of problems from within its own constituency. For all
our traditional explanations of Christian belief make sense in the
context of the worldview of modernity and the Enlightenment.
Christians have assumed that Descartes was right, and have taken it
for granted that the exercise of human reason is the way to understand things. We have been through a long history of preferring
secondary means of knowing God through Bible reading, sermons,
books, theology, hymns and so on, in the conscious effort to try and
make spirituality something that is both reasonable (the Greek
paradigm) and practical (the Roman heritage). But whatever spirituality may ultimately turn out to be, it is neither of those two
things. Hand in hand with this emphasis on what is rational there
has typically been a distrust of the emotions and intuitions as an
appropriate vehicle for divine truth. Further, because both rationality and faith have historically been defined as such by men, the
church has been dominated by men and male ways of thinking and
being. Beyond that, and as a consequence of it, it has been taken for
granted that adult ways of perceiving God are the right ones
(thereby marginalizing children), and that Western ways of being
are the best possible ones (therefore the gospel has too often found
itself used as a prop in support of the values of white, Western
people). All this poses a major problem for the church, not this time
from outside, but from within its own membership. For today's
Christians are in effect straddling two cultures. Their daily lives are
predominantly lived out within the developing culture of

post-modernity, which they are embracing for all the same reasons as other people are. But within the church they find themselves confronted with an almost totally different culture. It is not so much that they struggle to face up to the demands of the gospel. They actually strain to know what the challenge of the gospel might be, because church often seems to operate in different ways than they know how to cope with. At a very simple level, this can be a communication question: the church is generally at home with words and cognitive concepts, whereas in the rest of life people make sense of things with images and symbols. To fit into the church culture, people need to have the ability to process ideas in abstractions in their heads – and fewer and fewer people actually know how to do that, including the church's traditional supporters in the educated middle classes.

On all the indicators that I can identify, the church seems to have committed itself so fully to the worldview of the Enlightenment that, now that is collapsing with accelerating speed, the church as an essentially conservative institution is being left behind by the pace of change, and is finding it increasingly difficult to be taken seriously by the new emerging mainstream Western culture. It is argued by some that the church's love affair with modernity was a self-conscious missiological engagement rather than a whole-hearted acceptance of the Enlightenment worldview. William Storrar, for example, defends the church's record as 'a brilliant accommodation with the modern world. For the best of missiological reasons, it married modernity' – a metaphor which can be utilized to explain the church's present predicament in terms of the end of 'a long and happy marriage with modernity . . . which has left it grief-stricken in the widowhood of postmodernity . . . It is not so much declining numerically as declining to come to terms with that loss, spiritually and theologically'.[12] There is a degree of truth in that analysis, and the marriage metaphor is certainly a useful one. But the church is struggling with more than just an inability to engage with the emerging cultural reality: for the most part it is actually resisting such engagement and (so far as the church

---

[12] William Storrar, 'From Braveheart to Faint-heart: Worship and Culture in Postmodern Scotland', in B. D. Spinks and I. R. Torrance (eds), *To Glorify God: Essays on Modern Reformed Liturgy* (Edinburgh: T. & T. Clark, 1999), 69–84; quotations are from pp. 78 and 79.

Establishment is concerned) not infrequently marginalizing those Christians who are seeking new ways to contextualize the faith in post-modern culture. If the church's only interest in modernity had been missiological, it would not have found it so difficult to leave it behind and move on to new missiological possibilities. The reality is, however, that the church does, for the most part, seem to like the culture of modernity, and espouses its values as if they were in some absolute sense the truth.

Of course, it is not hard to appreciate why it should seem attractive to imagine that the church engaged with modernity only as a missiological tactic, because that then neatly absolves our forebears from complicity with the oppressive and exploitational aspects of modernity, as seen in the effects of colonialism and globalization. But this kind of argument simply does not match the facts, either in relation to Christendom as classically conceived, or in relation to the rearguard action on behalf of modernity in which many Christians are still engaged. The fact is that from a missiological perspective, the church's problem is to be located precisely in its unthinking acceptance of the essentially secular values of the Enlightenment. That is unquestionably the tap root from which most of the present difficulties stem, whether in relation to empowering Christians to live in ways that will bear witness to gospel values, or developing appropriate ways of sharing faith with unchurched people.

However, that statement – true though it is – needs some further qualification. For in our eagerness to distance ourselves from the mistaken excesses of the past, we must also remember the positive side of what has gone before. Take, for example, the emphasis on reason, and the consequent insistence that faith needs to have a rational foundation. A couple of generations ago that led to the conclusion that, in religious terms, nothing could possibly be worth believing. With the questioning of that outlook, much contemporary speculation on spirituality seems to have swung to the opposite extreme, and we now live in a culture – most obviously exemplified by the New Age – where everything and anything seems to be worth believing, and for some people the more bizarre and unlikely it is on the rational level, then the more value there is in believing it. Bearing witness to faith in a generation that is increasingly attracted to the irrational as an alternative to materialist rationalism might need to begin by underlining the importance of thinking. Being rational about things is not necessarily the same as being a rationalist – nor for that matter is irrationality the only alternative to an over-confident rationalism. There is more to the human personality than a left-brained analytical understanding of things, and the non-rational or right-brained side of ourselves, as experienced and expressed through feeling and imagination, is undoubtedly more important than Western people have typically allowed. But if we depend only on our non-rational intuitions for everything it is all too easy to misrepresent and misunderstand things in a way that will effectively undermine any serious spiritual search for truth. Many people today seem unable to tell the difference between fact and fantasy, and bearing witness to the gospel in our generation might need to begin with an insistence that there are at least *some* objective realities out there! The critical attitude engendered by the Enlightenment emphasis on reason is far from being all bad news!

Having said that, however, it is undeniable that on the whole Christians have related to the forces of modernity and Enlightenment in a very uncritical way. They have accepted without question its weaknesses as well as (even more than) its strengths, and the impact of this, especially now we are faced with a fast-changing cultural context, is devastating. In its ways of knowing and definitions of what is worth knowing, not to mention prevailing attitudes to anything remotely mystical, numinous or supernatural, much of Western Christianity looks increasingly like one of the final resting places of a rationalist-materialist worldview which has been rejected by just about everyone else. As a consequence the church often has a fragmented vision of itself, and its theology and spirituality suffer from a cognitive captivity that inhibits the development of a truly holistic gospel that will speak authentically to the needs of people in a post-modern world.

## Finding a New Way

Clearly, we have a lot of baggage to sort through in order to find ways of articulating the gospel effectively for the twenty-first century. The one thing that is clear to me is that we will require a much more extensive spiritual tool kit than we have been accustomed to using in the past.

Social psychologist Abraham Maslow is credited with having once observed that 'If the only tool you have is a hammer, you tend to see every problem as if it was a nail' – and that fairly sums up where the church finds itself. We have only one tool – or, more accurately, several different models of what is the same basic tool. They are all oriented toward rational, cognitive, left-brained ways of doing things. Using a hammer to remove a screw is a very difficult enterprise – not impossible, maybe, but definitely not recommended, and if you try it there is a high risk that you will damage the wood, destroy the screw and quite possibly harm yourself into the bargain. The analogy holds good in the church. Older people, who were educated in a system which saw everything as decided by human reason, and which required everything to be clearly classified and systematized, often simply cannot understand the concerns and questions of younger people who are truly a part of post-modern culture – and 'older' in this context means roughly people over forty. Raised and educated in a different generation, they find it hard to comprehend the extent to which reason is no longer dominant in today's world. Shirley Maclaine's view that 'It seems to be all about feeling, not thinking'[13] has been referred to already in an earlier chapter, but in truth she is quite benevolent to the culture of modernity, and there are many others who want to go much further. Today, a general distrust of reason is widespread in academia, largely through the influence of Jacques Derrida who has argued that what he calls 'logocentrism' (the objectification of words and reason) is the major source of discontinuity in Western culture, and that there is no such thing as objective reality, only different perceptions of what is 'real' for different people.[14]

Nor is all this merely a matter of arcane speculation relevant only to those who are attracted by such debates: on the contrary, it is central to the church's mission at this time in history. Philosophy professor Jacob Needleman is perhaps a classic example of today's spiritual searcher, who is not against the church or Christianity, but

---

[13] Shirley Maclaine, *Out on a Limb* (London: Bantam, 1983), 215.

[14] Significant works are J. Derrida, *Writing and Difference*, translated by Alan Bass (Chicago: University of Chicago Press, 1978); *Margins of Philosophy*, translated by Alan Bass (Chicago: University of Chicago Press, 1982).

cannot see its relevance because it is 'only a matter of words, exhortations and philosophy rather than a matter of practical guidance for experiencing directly the truth of the teachings . . . We are looking for the Christianity that works, that actually produces real change in human nature, real transformation.'[15] Needleman wrote that back in 1980, but George Barna discovered exactly the same concern among young adults in his 1994 study of what in the USA are called 'baby busters' (people born between 1965 and 1983). He reports an interview with a twenty-year-old called Lisa Baker, who commented:

> I honestly tried the churches, but they just couldn't speak to me. I'm not against churches or religion. I just don't want to waste my time in places that have no real wisdom, only to discover that when I'm fifty or something. All I want is reality. Show me God. Help me to understand why life is the way it is, and how I can experience it more fully and with greater joy. I don't want the empty promises. I want the real thing. And I'll go wherever I find that truth system.[16]

Later on, he concludes that 'Busters believe what they can feel, taste, see, hear, and touch – and very little else.'[17] All my own experience points in exactly the same direction. But in the average church, how much is there to feel, taste, see, hear and touch?

Of course, some will ask, how much should there be? As with most other questions related to this theme, there could be a long and complex answer to that. But for a biblical reference point, we could do worse than reflect on the fact that when Jesus was asked to summarize his message, he quoted the book of Deuteronomy to the effect that 'you shall love the Lord your God with all your heart, and with all your soul, and with all your mind, and with all your strength . . . you shall love your neighbour as yourself' (Mark 12:30–31). Both parts of that statement are important, but the first part is particularly relevant to this discussion, for whatever else may be said, it

---

[15] Jacob Needleman, *Lost Christianity* (Garden City, NY: Doubleday, 1980), 4, 35.

[16] George Barna, *Baby Busters: The Disillusioned Generation* (Chicago: Northfield, 1994), 93.

[17] Barna, *Baby Busters*, 69.

presents a holistic vision of discipleship that has largely been sidelined in traditional Western Christianity. We have done a wonderful job of loving God with our minds, while to varying degrees we have either dismissed altogether or been embarrassed by the possibilities of a spirituality that expresses itself through the heart (a broad biblical concept, but certainly including the emotions), or the spirit (harder to define, but definitely something mystical and/or numinous), or the strength (physical bodies). Thinking and rational processes are not unimportant, but even on a simplistic view of what Jesus is saying, that only constitutes 25 per cent of the total demand of the gospel. Whereas we typically offer people something to think about, the kind of all-embracing discipleship of which Jesus speaks is an invitation to explore a balanced spirituality that engages every part of the human personality. If the church is to be effective in communicating the gospel today, it will be through the rediscovery of that holistic balance. In particular, we will need to affirm that spirituality comes before theology, and allow experience of God to take precedence over metaphysical speculation. After all, in the New Testament, following Jesus is the first act, and reflecting on the meaning and significance of that following comes subsequently. Moreover, we will need to insist that this is no newfangled notion dreamed up by a few trendy new-millennium theologians. Not only can such teaching be traced back to Jesus himself, but it can also be found in the classic Western theological tradition. Anselm of Canterbury (1033–1109), for example, put it this way: 'I do not seek to understand in order that I may believe, but I believe in order that I may understand. For this also do I believe: that "I shall not understand unless I believe".'[18] Today's Christians will be judged more by the quality of their spirituality than by the truth of their message. I am not saying that truth is not important – but our entire inherited understanding of the nature of 'truth', and the apologetic we have used to establish it, seem to me to be derived from the insights and using the tools of an essentially secular worldview that is rooted in rationalist materialism. For me, that would raise questions even if people were making enquiries that could be addressed in that way. But on the whole, they are not, and most spiritual searchers are not first asking

---

[16] Anselm, *Proslogion* 1.

whether Christianity is true in some absolute sense, but what difference it might make to them if they choose to follow Jesus. If they come and follow Jesus, how will that impact lives and help people be more fulfilled human beings?

Discerning how to address questions like that, while being faithful to Jesus, is more fully explored in my book *Faith in a Changing Culture*. I have argued there that a fundamental need will be the rediscovery of community as a central part of Christian faith and practice, and a realignment of the relationship between theology and spirituality. This will be a huge challenge to the *status quo*, for it will require us to put into reverse gear the way most of our churches operate. We typically invite people to believe first (accept the creeds, sign statements of faith or, more simply, but nevertheless cognitively, 'believe in Jesus') – and then, we say, you can belong to the community of God's people. The need of our culture, however (not to mention the gospel imperative itself), is for us to create a community where people can feel comfortable to belong, and then to be continuously challenging and encouraging one another in the belonging and following. Moreover, I have argued that far from this being a mere accommodation of the gospel to the spirit of the age, it is actually a more biblical way of being church, deeply rooted not only in the teaching of Jesus himself, but in the fundamental Christian doctrines of creation and incarnation (for it will be no more advantageous for the church to marry post-modernism than it was for a previous generation to fall in love with modernity).

One of the interesting features of this present moment is that many lines of research seem to be converging to point to appropriate ways forward through which the church might engage with today's rising culture and the spiritual search which is an integral part of it. I have tackled it here largely from the standpoint of the history of ideas. But several studies aimed at identifying the felt needs of ordinary people are pointing in the same direction. In the survey of young adults already mentioned, George Barna observed that

> the spiritual journey of [today's generation] is based upon a desire to grow personally through the discovery of personally beneficial truths and practices. *What most churches and religious organizations fail to offer is a tangible means of becoming a more completely whole individual.* The religious faiths that will win . . . support . . . are those which enhance relation-

ships and lifestyles . . . Allowing a faith to be positioned as a series of rules, traditions, or punishments is antithetical to the search . . . *A faith that becomes positioned as a means of growing personally through deeper relationships and understanding would be more attractive.*[19]

A British survey carried out by the Christian Research Association on behalf of Churches Together in England reached almost identical conclusions, namely that unchurched people 'are more interested in relationships than in receiving information about God or church . . . need churches that are caring – not just friendly . . . are more likely to respond to churches that are interested, than to those that are interesting . . . are looking for relevance, not history . . . want practical answers to life's hard questions'.[20]

## Post-modern Ministry

There are at least two ways of addressing the question of what the church will need to be in the new cultural context. One is to accept the culture in which we operate, and reassess the nature of ministry so as to contextualize the faith within that paradigm. The other is to attempt to resist cultural change, or at least to pour scorn on what is manifestly happening. This latter notion is one to which many Christians will pay lip-service, though if the earlier analysis of the relationship between church and modernity is even half accurate, it is the exact opposite of what Christians have actually done. Either way, we need to take account of what is happening in our culture: 'Trends, like horses, are easier to ride in the direction they are already going . . . You may decide to buck the trend, but it is still helpful to know it is there.'[21]

On my understanding, the trends of today's culture are clearly away from the inherited models of ministry (which go back well beyond the Reformation, to Christendom, and further back still into the organizational structures of the Roman Empire).[22] If there

---

[19] Barna, *Baby Busters*, 150–151; emphasis added.

[20] *Finding Faith in 1994* (London: CRA, 1995).

[21] John Naisbitt and Patricia Aburdene, *Megatrends* (New York: Warner, 1982), xxxii.

[22] For a judicious assessment of selected aspects of such cultural influences, cf. John Finney, *Recovering the Past: Celtic and Roman Mission* (London: Darton Longman & Todd, 1996).

are historical antecedents for something like post-modern society, then the Hellenistic social matrix of New Testament times would have a good claim to be such – which ought actually to be good news for the church. It suggests to me that we would be wise to accept the reality of cultural change – not by using it slavishly as a model which the church ought to copy, but rather as a mirror through which we can see reflected not only how we now are in relation to the wider spiritual concerns of our day, but also how with God's help, and in the light of Scripture, we might now become in order to be effective witnesses to Jesus Christ. My personal view would be that we can therefore learn much from models of ministry in the earliest Christian communities. There has been no shortage of books and articles written on the nature of ministry in the churches of the New Testament period, and no useful purpose will be served by repeating or reviewing it all here.[23] Rather, I want to focus on the way in which these insights can be applied in relation to the changing cultural scene of today and tomorrow.

I have no doubt that in the new paradigm, 'ministry' in the broad sense will be more important than 'ministers' in the narrow, more traditional sense. But there will still be people who are employed by the churches, which is why it is appropriate to address the question by asking who they will be, and how they will operate. Let me present my observations in a series of statements that highlight the differences there will be between the ministers of yesterday and their counterparts tomorrow.

*In terms of their own personal and spiritual formation, tomorrow's pastors will need to be relational, not hierarchical.* One of the first changes will actually be in the terminology which church workers use to describe themselves, for traditional words like 'minister' or 'priest' will not appropriately reflect the emerging nature of relevant ministry. Both those terms originate from within a hierarchical notion of culture, and they communicate that image to the outside world. We will need to find other terminology, and my own preference would be the image of 'pastor'. This already has a place

---

[23] For especially useful insights, see Robert Banks, *Paul's Idea of Community* (Peabody, MA: Hendrickson, 2nd edn, 1994); David L. Bartlett, *Ministry in the New Testament* (Minneapolis: Fortress Press, 1993).

in the heritage of some church traditions, notably the Roman Catholic Church and in some independent churches. This will need to be more than a semantic change, however, for tomorrow's pastors will need to be prepared to minister alongside and with people, rather than to or at them. Rather than being people of single-minded commitment to their theological task, they will be people of compassion, who know when abstract principles are inadequate to match the realities of people's everyday lives. They will be spiritual soul-mates rather than spiritual directors. There will need to be what C. Jeff Woods has called a move 'From Reasonable Spirituality to Mysterious Spirituality'.[24] That will require pastors who will themselves be whole individuals – as happy with intuition and imagination, art and creativity, mysticism and the supernatural, as they are with books, words, and theology. They will take Jesus as their model rather than choosing role models from church history.[25] In the process, they might find themselves in conflict with their churches' preconceived expectations of what their 'professional' workers should be like. But they will need to persevere, for in the end (and probably sooner rather than later) even the establishment will realize that they are its only hope for survival.

*Tomorrow's pastors will have a strong and positive self-image, enabling them to work as partners with all God's people.* They will need to be 'strong partners' rather than 'strong leaders', community builders not empire builders. They will know how to work with people in genuine dialogue, being listeners as well as speakers. They will not believe that only they have access to the word of God, nor that God can only be known through the gifts of professional ministry. They will not be spiritual drill sergeants, operating from a position above other believers, nor will they see themselves as beneath other people ('servants'). Being neither above nor below means they will be alongside others, sharing their gifts and insights but not

---

[24] The title of chapter 6 in C. Jeff Woods, *Congregational Megatrends* (Bethesda, MD: Alban Institute, 1996).

[25] There is a natural temptation to look to previous generations who were apparently less embarrassed by the mystical and numinous than we seem to be (some of the Puritans, for instance). But the nature of the paradigm shift beyond which we now operate severely limits the ways in which we can usefully learn from the past (as distinct from taking comfort from the fact that, in all times, there have been those who bucked the trend).

preaching at them.[26] The question whether pastors have 'authority', and if so what kind of 'authority', has become redundant and irrelevant in the context of the new paradigm. Pastors of the future will be less interested in 'teaching' others than in learning for themselves in the company of others. They will have skills in planning and leadership that are open-ended, not prescriptive. They will know how to be part of the construction team that will build faith communities beginning from the raw materials available (people as well as ideas), rather than assembling a pre-packaged item. Their understanding of what it means to be 'church' will not come out of a box, like furniture made from a kit, but out of a woodyard full of timber of different shapes, sizes, and textures.[27]

*In methods of working, tomorrow's pastors will not be lone individuals.* In the aftermath of a worldview which gave too much credence to reductionism as a way of understanding things, our culture is no longer tolerant of methodologies which pigeon-hole people in separate compartments. One of the major practical criticisms of allowing reason to dominate is that it provided the tools with which some of the most damaging conflicts of modern times could be set up

---

[26] They may well not be preaching any sermons at all as we know them today, for preaching in the mode we are now familiar with is itself a product of Renaissance rhetoric. Cf. the comment of William Abraham: ' . . . we need to abandon the image of proclamation that is so prevalent in the modern Protestant tradition. That image, represented by the solid, tripartite sermon . . . is a culturally relative phenomenon' (*The Logic of Evangelism* [London: Hodder & Stoughton, 1989], 171). Walter Wink goes further and describes the sermon as a 'paradigm of modernity' (*Transforming Bible Study* [Nashville: Abingdon Press, 1990], 74). For some biblical parameters within which to address this question, see my *Faith in a Changing Culture* (London: HarperCollins, 1997), 128–135.

[27] The inability of pastors to work in genuine partnership with others is well documented as a major reason for the decline of many churches. Cf. Michael J. Fanstone, *The Sheep That Got Away* (Tunbridge Wells: MARC, 1993), and William D. Hendricks, *Exit Interviews: Revealing Stories of Why People Are Leaving the Church* (Chicago: Moody, 1993); Philip Richter and Leslie J. Francis, *Gone but not Forgotten* (London: Darton Longman & Todd, 1998) – all of which highlight this as a major problem. Kennon Callahan observes that actions, not words, are required, complaining of 'pastors who talk a pretty good game of "theology of the laity", when in fact they are unwilling to share their authority with their laity. The direct result is the weakening of leadership resources and a decreased sense of accomplishment in mission and program' (*Twelve Keys to an Effective Church* [San Francisco: HarperCollins, 1983], 47).

– dichotomies between white people and black people, between women and men, between Aryans and Jews, between people and the natural world, etc. The mood of our culture is to bring things together in holistic harmony, not to keep them separated in different compartments (something which is rejected as being essentially a means of control and domination). This should be good news for Christians who take the New Testament seriously! In terms of practical ministry, though, it undoubtedly raises some challenges that today's ecclesiastical structures might prefer not to address.

For tomorrow's pastors will be women and men from different theological and denominational backgrounds working together in partnership. Some churches will find this hard to accept, on both counts. Even those who think they have resolved issues over women's ministry and ecumenical co-operation have mostly not grasped the real issue which the changing cultural paradigm is presenting. Those churches which have admitted women to their ministry have typically seen it in terms of allowing women to do jobs that previously were reserved only for men – but the actual nature of the jobs available has still been defined according to a male understanding of what ministry actually is. As a consequence, the notion of 'ministry' is still generally patriarchal, even when women are included – being committed to the perpetuation of the very same hierarchical cultural agenda which post-modernism has questioned and is in the process of ditching. In cultural terms, a church which does not ask very fundamental questions about the nature of ministry simply will not survive for much longer. Its main priority will need to be the tidy management of its own extinction – and unless something changes very quickly, that is where several of our mainline denominations are already heading. The day of the solo 'professional' minister is at an end, and in that context even legitimate arguments about things like whether that solo minister should be a man or a woman are simply irrelevant. The same could be said of ecumenical collaboration in ministry. The traditional way of formulating the questions is no longer a relevant and meaningful way of addressing the issue: the paradigm shift has actually changed the terms of reference within which the nature of ministry needs to be understood.

*Tomorrow's pastors will be flexible in ministry and diverse in lifestyle.* The pastors of tomorrow may well operate more like 'pastoral consultants', shared among a number of neighbouring congregations, to facilitate, empower and train lay people. They will not be the pastor *to* these lay people, but will help them work out for themselves how to be the people of God.[28] This kind of role will be facilitated by changing life patterns among church members, who will follow trends in the culture at large, which are moving towards defining personal identity and purpose less by reference to full-time employment, and more in terms of 'leisure' activities. For Christians that means church (in sociological terms = leisure) will meet a different need and lead to a different style of commitment than has typically been the case for church members of previous generations. Those who stick with the church will increasingly want to support it with more than just cash. In the short and medium term, changes in the world of work mean that more people will have to construct their own 'designer lifestyles', whether they like it or not – and for Christians, their ministry within the church will be one major component of this. Existing opportunities for early retirement have already highlighted the potential in this trend, but it will only accelerate and become the norm at all stages of life.[29] There are many reasons for this fundamental shift, not least the uncertainty and unpredictability of cultural change itself, and a natural desire for people to have sufficient flexibility in their lives to be able to protect their most precious resource of all – time – and not be trapped in enterprises that will not be rewarding and worthwhile. Traditional missionary-sending agencies are already seeing a major shift of emphasis from the career-missionary to short-term placements, and the same trend is discernible in many churches with the emergence of non-stipendiary ministries and the like. In my opinion, the most effective pastors in tomorrow's church will themselves share in this kind of flexible lifestyle, and for many, pastoral work may not be lifelong, and it may not be full-time.

*Tomorrow's pastors will be missionary pastors.* They will be well equipped to minister to people outside the church, not exclusively to those within it. For several centuries past, church and society were almost one and the same thing, and when society was fully supportive of the church, the church saw no need to minister to the

---

[28] Cf. Woods, *Congregational Megatrends*, 103–120.
[29] Cf. Charles Handy, *The Empty Raincoat* (London: Hutchinson, 1994).

society. The door was open, and anyone wanting the services of the church could – and did – walk through it. In that context, maintenance ministry was appropriate. Today things are quite different, and pastors who do not know how to minister to the unchurched are mostly supervising the closure of their churches, and the disappearance of their own livelihood along with them. Kennon Callahan identifies the challenge quite clearly:

> The day of the professional minister is over . . . [that model] may be functional in a reasonably churched culture. But . . . is lost on a mission field. Professional ministers are at their best (and they do excellent work) in a churched culture. But put them in an unchurched culture, and they are lost. In an unchurched culture, they do a reasonably decent job of presiding over stable and declining and dying churches. They maintain a sense of presence, dignity, decorum, and decency – with a quietly sad regret – much like the thoughtful undertaker who sees to keeping things in good order throughout the funeral.[30]

## Theological Education

Inevitably, these trends will have repercussions for the way people are trained for ministry. Our next chapter examines this in more detail, but in order to provide a clear focus for that, it will be worth noting here four major consequences that will follow from this emerging pattern of effective ministry for the new century:

- Theological education will need to take place in an international and ecumenical context, paying at least as much attention to non-Western as to Western theology and ways of being church. Furthermore, it will need to find ways of taking account of the theological insights of the whole people of God, and integrating them as of equal value with the opinions of those who might regard themselves as 'professional theologians'.

---

[30] Kennon L. Callahan, *Effective Church Leadership* (San Francisco: HarperCollins, 1990), 3–4.

- Alongside this will go an integration of what are now different theological disciplines. Instead of being discipline-led, theological education will be issues-led, with appropriate insights being drawn together into a holistic synthesis from biblical studies, church history, theological reflection and church praxis. This is an inevitable consequence of the move towards 'designer lifestyles', as people bring their experience of the marketplace and seek to understand the relevance of the Bible, or systematic theology, or church history, to it all. In this context, practical or applied theology will no longer be an additional or optional extra but becomes the focus that gives meaning and purpose to everything else – 'the crown of theological studies,' as Schleiermacher called it.[31]

- Affective approaches to learning will have equal status alongside cognitive understanding. The arts, creativity, and spirituality will transform the personal formation of pastoral workers beyond all recognition.[32]

- Theological education will be a lifelong cyclical process of reflection on experience, and in the light of ongoing praxis, and much of this will probably take place 'on the job' rather than on the campuses of theological colleges.

---

[31] F. D. Schleiermacher, *Brief Outline on the Study of Theology* (Richmond VA: John Knox Press 1966), 27 (originally in German 1830). Cf. the work of Don Browning who, starting from a different place entirely, carefully argues for the same realignment of theological disciplines: *A Fundamental Practical Theology* (Minneapolis: Fortress Press 1991).

[32] Cf. the comment of M. D. Chenu, that 'The greatest tragedy in theology in the past three centuries has been the divorce of the theologian from the poet, the dancer, the musician, the painter, the dramatist, the actress, the movie-maker...' (quoted in M. Fox, *Original Blessing* [Santa Fe: Bear & Co., 1983], 180).

# Chapter 7

# Theological Education for the Third Millennium[1]

In the light of all that has been said in previous chapters, it will come as no surprise to know that the way theology is traditionally taught today – indeed the very concept of what theology is – has (like everything else) been shaped and influenced by historical and philosophical trends within Western civilization. The culture stemming from the European Enlightenment, and including all that is now identified as modernity, has had a profound and far-reaching impact on theological education. Until recently, educational theorists in most disciplines accepted without question the Enlightenment assumptions about what is worth knowing, and therefore how it might be taught. These influences have typically come from three main philosophical premises: rationalism, which in educational terms tends to affirm that the only things worth knowing are what we can think about in particular analytical, abstract ways; materialism, which assumes that the only things worth thinking about are what we can see, touch and handle; and reductionism, which leads to the conclusion that things can best be understood by taking them to pieces. The widespread adoption of such ideas has made a significant contribution to the present crisis in modernity, and it is inevitable that as a result many aspects of the educational model arising from this paradigm are being questioned, in many disciplines.

[1] An earlier version of this chapter appeared in the *British Journal of Theological Education* 6/3 (1994–95), 3–8, though it has been very considerably expanded here.

With minor variations, however, theological education still generally operates within the old paradigm. Depending on where they would wish to place themselves on the theological spectrum, different colleges and seminaries might find themselves more inclined to one axis than to the others: conservative and evangelical Protestants, for example, are more likely to be rationalists, while more liberal mainline Christians might be somewhat more influenced by materialism – though reductionism is a *sine qua non* for everyone. Theological education is consequently fragmented and compartmentalized into different disciplines that often have no idea how to speak to each other, and being educated has come to be identified with the ability to dissect and analyse knowledge. There is little sense of holistic learning and all too often we are producing graduates who cannot integrate either faith or personal development with what they think they know about theology. While there is no one simple answer to the increasing problem of clergy burn-out, this lack of integration in the way we train people for ministry is certainly a major contributory factor, and when church leaders find it difficult to relate faith and life in meaningful ways, we can be sure that one consequence of that will be dysfunction within the context of the local Christian community within which they serve.

Church culture itself, of course, has traditionally operated within the same secular model of reality, with discipleship predominantly understood in terms of doctrinal and theological knowledge and commitments. Relatively few churches give much place to the numinous or mystical, and as a result Christian faith has become an essentially cognitive activity, focusing on what people believe in an intellectual sort of way. No doubt this is why Western churches are increasingly finding that their ways of doing things appeal only to certain limited sections of the population, namely those who process information in an analytical, cerebral fashion. I hope that previous chapters will have said enough to demonstrate that if we continue down this track, not only will it turn out to be institutionally suicidal for the church as we know it, but it is also at odds with some central values of the gospel itself, not least the doctrine of the incarnation, through which Christians affirm that 'the Word became flesh'. It is relatively easy to make the diagnosis, but those of us who are engaged in the task of theological education also need to take seriously our own pivotal position in enabling church leaders to develop sustainable models that will be relevant to the demand for effective mission and spiritual nurture in contemporary culture, while remaining firmly rooted in the historical tradition of the church's faith. That is not to say that what goes on in theological education will be determinative of whatever future the church in the West might have: to do that would be to over-indulge ourselves and underestimate the grace of God. But it is a simple fact that most church leaders model themselves after the style of those who taught them, which means that if our churches are indeed perceived as irrelevant to the spiritual search by the population at large, those of us who have trained their leaders need to shoulder some of the blame, and think creatively about how we might empower future generations not only to understand the cultural predicament in which we find ourselves, but also to move forward in effective ways.

## New Directions

If we were to begin with a clean sheet, and redesign theological education from nothing, many factors would need to be given serious consideration. Not least, we might wish to ask whether theological colleges and seminaries as we know them would be the best place to start. I suspect that in the medium term the cultural changes now taking place will force us to address that question, whether we like it or not. But for the moment I want to begin with what we have, recognizing that most of our institutions are already so hard pressed in financial terms that they are unlikely to be easily convinced that they can afford the luxury of reinventing themselves from top to bottom. So what questions can we realistically address, given our present starting points? I want to propose here that there are four main areas of theological education that could be addressed in ways that would not only enhance the quality of the theological enterprise itself, but would also equip church leaders to feel more comfortable with the new challenges that they now face as they seek to contextualize the gospel in post-modern culture.

## Redefining theology

We desperately need to develop a more holistic model of theology itself. It is not that we lack a broadly based theological foundation – indeed, any half-decent institution will already include in its curriculum study of the Bible, church history, systematic theology, practical theology (which should include especially understanding of the nature of cultural change) and the study of non-Christian spiritual traditions (which, to be relevant, needs to be defined more widely than just other major world faiths). But the problem is that all too often these subjects are each pursued as if none of the others existed, or was important. In many institutions it is possible to study the Bible, for instance, without ever giving any consideration as to how its message might be communicated to the average person who is already a church member, let alone the millions who are not. Hermeneutics, if it features at all, too easily becomes yet another exercise in speculative philosophy, while courses in ostensibly practical subjects such as homiletics or pastoral care all too often operate in a way that takes little or no account of what has been learned in courses on the Bible or systematic theology. For example, if the traditional source-critical understanding of the origins of the synoptic gospels is correct (that Matthew and Luke used Mark, plus material from the hypothetical source Q, supplemented by material unique to each of them), then it should presumably make a difference to the way church leaders help other people to understand those texts. Yet all too often, no connections at all are made, and the way they go on to use the gospels in church life bears little or no relationship to what students have been taught in New Testament classes.

If anything, there is an even more obvious lack of integration between the study of theology and personal spirituality. As a teacher of practical theology, I am perhaps especially aware of the attitude found in some circles, that anything practical is really the Cinderella of theological education, and that the truly serious stuff is concerned with the understanding of scriptural and other texts. But texts have never been ends in themselves: they are always produced by, and therefore reflect the opinions of, closely defined sections of any culture. However important the Bible may be, following Jesus is not an exercise in textual exegesis but is something that celebrates and permeates the whole of life. Personal experience, ritual and art are fundamental to faith communities, and expertise in textual studies will not of itself give insight and understanding into these crucial aspects of Christianity. In saying this, it is not my intention to denigrate or downplay traditional theological disciplines: I myself spent much of my life teaching the New Testament before moving into practical theology, and I find that my love for and understanding of the Bible plays a significant role in my thinking about the future course that the church now needs to take. But cognitive study should go hand in hand with affective understandings of faith, and taking this seriously will have far-reaching implications for the whole structure and rationale of theological education. Some theological educators are still struggling to come to terms with the current academic fashions of spelling out clear aims and objectives for what they teach, and even when they produce them, statements of purpose frequently tend to be about the transmission of information from professors' notes and/or textbooks to students' notes. Relatively few theological courses spell out objectives in educational terms, let alone in terms of goals for personal and spiritual maturity. But these are precisely the questions we should be asking – things like, 'What is this course actually for?' 'How will this equip people for effective ministry?' 'How will it facilitate personal growth, encourage faith and bring us closer to God?'

The need for education to foster development of the whole person is widely accepted today, and it is especially important in theological education. For one thing, growth into personal maturity is what the gospel is all about, enabling those who follow Christ to become 'mature people, attaining to the whole measure of the fullness of Christ' (Ephesians 4:13). In addition, however, people coming to theological education often bring with them unhappy experiences of church culture. In my experience, this is a growing trend as people who want to be serious about their faith find they are not being nurtured in their local church, and decide to study the subject more deeply in order to address that. For people like this, a central concern of theological education will need to be the fostering of a holistic spirituality which will enable personal growth to take place within a context of healing and forgiveness. This emerging need is both a result of, and an appropriate response to, our changing culture. In the past, virtually no one embarked on a course in theology (of all subjects) without first having a conscious sense of calling and commitment to a clearly defined career path which they then expected would occupy them for the rest of their lives. Today, even where full-time ministry is still available, it no longer has the status it once did, and the ambiguous relationship between church and culture is inevitably projected into the practice of ministry. The effects of all this are clearly evident in the sort of students who are now enrolling for courses in theology, and the kind of questions they bring with them. Instead of the single-minded commitment to lifelong ministry, which began from a settled faith, most students bring to their studies more questions than answers. They study theology not because they know who they are meant to be, but in order to find out. In the deepest sense, they study the subject not because they have a neatly packaged faith which they want to explore, but as part of the quest to find faith, and especially to discover what difference the gospel might make to the things they and their families wrestle with in everyday life.

To join students on such a journey is undoubtedly one of the greatest privileges that theological educators can have. But teachers should not underestimate the level of personal threat that this may present, for to accomplish it well we will ourselves be required to be more personally open than we have traditionally been encouraged to be. I am not unsympathetic to those who find themselves apprehensive about the consequences of such vulnerability, and who would prefer to continue to protect themselves behind lecterns and books – but that is not the way in which we will make the most useful contribution to the spiritual development of our students. Though individuals will no doubt struggle in their own way with this challenge, the very least that we all should be working towards is the provision of more learning opportunities which will offer scope for personal interaction, not to mention more variety in learning experiences, particularly the incorporation of right-brained or creative experiences. Alongside this will be a recognition that the teacher is not the only resource for learning, and that the student's own experience must be both recognized and valued as a key element within the total learning environment. To move in this direction, it may be necessary to allow some of the differentiation between discrete subject areas to break down, so that cross-fertilization can take place in a genuinely interdisciplinary way.

## Understanding the market

Many of the needs just identified are themselves related to the changing culture of Western life and the redefinition of Christian ministry that is taking place as part of this. Some of the ramifications of that were spelled out in the last chapter, where I suggested that ministry itself will need to become much more flexible and diverse than has been the case in the recent past. If my analysis there is even half correct, it stands to reason that there will be knock-on effects in relation to the future shape of theological education. No doubt churches will continue to speak of ministry as a vocation rather than a job, and may also insist that ministers are not employees of the church but are servants of God. If those are the kind of definitions the church finds itself able to live with, they probably do no particular harm – though it hardly commends the gospel if (as sometimes happens) they are used as a device for dodging accountability under laws designed to protect people from exploitation by their employers. In any case, the sociological reality of ministry, whether as vocation or job, is likely to be the same as for any other kind of employment. In the past, training for ministry was something that people underwent at the beginning of their career, and what they learned then carried them right through to the end. That is no longer the case in other areas of employment, and ministry is no different in this regard. Theological education is now recognized as a process of lifelong learning. Moreover, because the best theological education is more than just the imparting of information about ancient texts, events and ideas, but includes the development of spirituality and the encouragement of personal growth, it will not just be ministers or other full-time church staff who are attracted to it. With rapidly changing life patterns in the wider culture, particularly the emergence of 'designer' lifestyles, the actual quality of life has become much more important to us than it was to earlier generations. Instead of seeking satisfaction and personal identity through their paid employment, increasing numbers of people are looking for satisfaction through the things they do in their own time. A holistic approach to theology in this context will focus around a unifying of Christian experience with the rest of (secular) life. Though much lip-service has been paid to this, churches seem to offer few opportunities for their members actually to explore the integration of their lives in this way. It is striking that one of the criticisms most often levelled at the churches by those who drift into the New Age is the complaint that Christianity does not effectively provide a bridge between the sacred and the secular, but operates with a limited understanding of the spiritual which is, in practice, more or less restricted to what goes on in church services and rituals. This is a significant challenge in itself, but in the context of the growing market for theological education among lay people who will in the future be giving portions of their life to the church while not disengaging from other forms of 'secular' employment, it presents new opportunities. For these people, with wide life experience of their own, are unlikely to be attracted by traditional models of theological education, but will be looking for an integrated and spiritually formative learning experience. Since they will also be paying for it from their own resources, they will naturally choose those opportunities that are most likely to deliver value for money in this area.

The recognition of this growing need for a more integrated approach will also require colleges and seminaries to forge ever closer relationships with their natural constituency in the churches. This will have to go well beyond the kind of temporary placements for theological students that are already part of the scene. If ministry moves in the direction I am now envisaging, with more flexible commitments and responsibilities, and increasing numbers of people involved in church work as just one part of their lifestyle package, churches will want to see theological education being made more readily available for all their members, often on their own premises. This kind of thing is already happening to a limited extent, as parishes and denominational bodies establish structured training programmes that will equip ordinary lay people to live and work as Christians where they are. To be effective, though, such training has to happen in the same place as people's everyday life and work. Visionary theological educators will grasp this opportunity to work alongside and with the churches, rather than assuming that full-time education is the norm, therefore only a minority are likely to be interested, and that minority will automatically travel to a college's own campus for the experience. Some notable experiments along these lines are already taking place. For example, the Seattle Association for Theological Education was formed by an ecumenical coalition of local churches who then invited three institutions (Seattle Pacific University, Fuller Seminary and Regent College) to join them in developing programmes of theological education that would integrate into precisely the kind of market that I have been describing here and in the last chapter. In different ways, the various programmes of Theological Education by Extension (TEE) operating mostly in the non-Western world are also seeking to address the same need, for ways of learning about faith that are rooted in the local circumstances in which people find themselves, and which will empower them for effective ministry in that context, without having to leave it. This is a different dynamic from institutions merely making their courses available for distance learning and, in order to forge such partnerships, colleges and semi-naries will face tough choices here, for they are bound to lose some of their autonomy and sense of control over what constitutes an appropriate curriculum. They should of course be accountable to their own governing bodies and to their universities or other validating organizations – but they also have accountability to their wider constituency in the churches and, ultimately, to the world at large.

### Integrating with the educational context

Throughout the Western world, education is undergoing some major shifts of emphasis, and most of what has been said here about theological education can be mirrored in other fields of study. Those countries whose education systems have been based on the American model have always offered more flexible routes to learning than has been the case with those based on the traditional British model, but Britain is undergoing rapid change that will in the end probably bring us close to the USA.[2] Greater organizational flexibility is already being implemented, with modular course units that can be used by students as the building blocks with which, in

---

[2] Ironically, the American model developed out of a Scottish model, which also originally laid greater emphasis on flexibility and diversity than its English counterpart. Though traditional theological education in Scotland attempted to maintain a broad base for much of the twentieth century, it has gradually been subsumed within the English style, and insofar as there is creative experimentation within the British scene today, it is mostly taking place outside the traditional centres of theological learning.

effect, they can construct their own degrees. As part of this, the concept of what constitutes an academic year is in the process of being restructured as self-contained semesters replace the inherited pattern of a complete year consisting of three interconnected terms. Though some are resistant to all this, it is the only way in which the demand for flexibility can be accommodated. Indeed, to meet the new situation fully the changes will probably have to be more radical than they have been so far, with a wholesale restructuring of the year into two or three semesters, or four quarters, and the widespread use of intensive courses to enable people to gain course credits during periods of holiday from their other employments. This will also probably include greater flexibility in allowing credits for lifelong learning, as well as the award of credits for achievements in other forms of educational endeavour, in church life as well as in more formal educational contexts. This is all standard practice in theological seminaries in the USA, and for some of them has been one of the key factors in ensuring their continued survival in a cut-throat marketplace.

As well as educational structures, the actual way in which people expect to learn is also undergoing rapid and substantial change. Technology is already redefining the ways in which resources can be made available to students, not least in relation to how much time they spend on a campus in full-time study, and it is already possible to follow a complete degree course through the World Wide Web. If it is not to be left behind by the development of these international digital networks, British theological education will need to be a part of this revolution, as colleges form coalitions and partnerships not only among themselves but also (and of more strategic importance) with institutions in other parts of the world. I would inject a note of caution here, however, for I am not convinced that theological education – of all things – can actually be delivered through distance-learning modes without questioning its own integrity. Of course, computers are useful for all sorts of straightforward learning tasks, and may well become dominant as tools for exchanging information. But a key underlying theme of this entire book has been that the church has become less attractive to today's spiritual pilgrims precisely because they see it as overemphasizing cognitive, rational discourse, to the exclusion – or certainly the marginalization – of more affective ways of being. One of the contradictions of our culture is the tension between our distrust of other people and our desperate search for community – highlighted, perhaps, by the way increasing numbers of us can apparently relate perfectly easily to others through a computer screen, which is arguably one of the most detached and individualistic experiences imaginable. Nevertheless, given that much of the attraction of the New Age is connected with the search for personal acceptance in a community, and given that community is also at the heart of the gospel, it would be both evangelistically counter-productive and doctrinally anomalous to imagine that it is desirable – still less possible – to learn those things that are most important about theology without personal interaction with others who have embarked on the same journey. To facilitate students who will engage in full-time study only during summer semesters or quarters, or for the final part of their overall course, it will be necessary to develop learning pedagogies that go well beyond the expectations of how we currently define extension studies, by incorporating not only the transmission of information but providing mentoring and spiritual friendship as an integral part of the whole process.

### Rethinking the product

To move in the direction indicated here will require a major conceptual shift in defining the product that is on offer, and this is something that challenges both British and American systems. Traditionally, the essential marketable product of theological education has been regarded as the courses of study and the qualifications to which they lead. The model proposed here would not downplay the importance of that, but would regard courses and qualifications as a means, and not an end in themselves. In keeping with what I perceive to be the central values of the gospel itself, we should be regarding people as the basic product of the process, with a corresponding concern for spiritual formation and vocational integration as an integral component of theological understanding, and therefore with significant emphasis on a coherent fusion of these elements rather than the maintenance of a fragmented approach. In the past, colleges and seminaries have generally formulated their institutional policies by asking questions like, 'What kind of courses do we want to offer?' or 'What knowledge of theology will our graduates possess?' Those with an effective contribution to make to the future will instead ask themselves, 'What kind of graduates will our people be?' and 'What will be their special contribution to the life of the church in the next generation?' In the course of addressing that kind of question, we will also probably find ourselves needing to redefine what we understand by a 'good education' in this context, in particular by re-evaluating exactly what we think 'quality' might mean in theological education.

## New Styles

It is easy enough to discuss all this at the conceptual level. But what does it all mean in terms of what happens in the classroom? For the last ten years or so I have been experimenting with different styles of teaching and learning, in the effort to pin all this down to practicalities, and I want to illustrate one possible way forward on the basis of my experience. I should emphasize that in the changing cultural context in which we operate, there will probably be many different ways in which the learning environment can be reshaped in order to meet today's and tomorrow's needs. My own way will not be the only possible model, nor will it necessarily turn out to be the best. But I have used it now in two quite different Scottish universities, as well as in seminaries and theological colleges in the USA and Australia, and it was highlighted as a model of good practice in a 1996 report sponsored by the UK government's Scottish Higher Education Funding Council,[3] so I think I can say with some confidence that it works – and in more than one system.

The concept is both simple and radical, and perhaps the most obvious difference that might be observed by the outsider would be in the length of a typical class, which might be as long as four hours. Invariably, students who enrol for such a course do so tentatively,

---

[3] The ASSHE (Assessment Strategies in Scottish Higher Education) Project was carried out by a team of researchers from Napier University and the University of Edinburgh between 1994 and 1996, under the auspices of the Committee of Scottish Higher Education Principals and financed by the Scottish Higher Education Funding Council.

and with a fair degree of hesitation. On the one hand, they can see advantages in a class that meets for four hours once a week, instead of on four separate hours on different days. But at the same time, they struggle to imagine what such an experience might be like. Some of them find it hard enough to stay awake for a lecture lasting only fifty minutes, so the prospect of doing that for a few hours can be daunting. Though I have met professors who could easily talk non-stop for at least four hours, that is not something I would recommend for the sake of either teacher or students. The profitable and productive use of time is obviously very important, and indeed is at the heart of the success of this style of learning. Different institutions and subjects lend themselves to different forms of creative activity, and as I review my own notes from such classes I see an amazing diversity of experiences, including role play, small-group work, watching videos and talking about them, story-telling, worship and prayer in many different interactive forms, making collages, plenaries, learning practical skills – and even elements that might look like traditional lectures, but which will typically be utilized as a point for extempore summing-up of what has already been discovered by other means. In addition, one or two structured coffee breaks always need to be built into any session as long as four hours – though even that can make a distinctive contri-bution. Maybe a few questions for reflection will be suggested at the start of the coffee break, and many students find that going off to talk in the coffee bar will give them a different kind of freedom from what they have even in the open setting of the class itself. When the class tutor joins them, other residual relational barriers can also be broken down. One university class I have taught in this format met from 12 noon to 4 pm, and therefore included lunchtime, and the sharing of food in that context itself became an important aspect of the inner dynamic of the group.

To date, I have developed six course units that are regularly being taught along these lines: two on the New Testament (one on the gospels, another on the epistles), and a further four in Practical Theology (*Spirituality and Creativity for Evangelism and Worship*; *Creative Arts and the Bible*; *Theological and Pastoral Perspectives on the Contemporary Family*; and *The Church in Contemporary Society*). I have been sufficiently encouraged by student feedback from around the world to be able to identify several quite specific advantages in this approach, which I believe are addressing the concerns identified in the first half of this chapter.

### Finding new ways of being

Since students tend to model themselves on those who teach them, and in view of the desperate need for our churches to find new ways of being church, one of the most urgent demands of the moment is for us to identify a new style of being that will meet the need of our culture as well as reflect gospel values. My consistent experience in many contexts has been that within this frame of reference class members interact with one another in a completely different way from how they do in classes lasting only for an hour or so. An atmosphere of mutual support is an important part of any educational process, and also – as any teacher will confirm – one of the most difficult things to engender. I am convinced that a major key to this is not so much the total number of hours students spend together in classes, but the way those hours are structured. Except in circumstances where people know one another very intimately to begin with, groups regularly spend the first 40 to 50 minutes getting the feel of one another and the mood of the occasion – and only after that do they begin to feel at ease, and unwind in such a way that new and creative experiences can take place. When the occasion itself is limited to only 60 minutes, that leaves very little prospect of any interaction that will move people on to deep learning or personal growth. But with more time, even a group who find it hard to relate to each other are liable to unwind a bit more. For most people, with two or three more hours available the quality of the time and the group experience increases on an exponential curve, and I have never taught a class like this which did not become a genuine community within (at most) three meetings. An unexpected bonus in terms of modelling new ways of being is that a class as long as four hours can very easily be taught by a team, or by two people in partnership. Team-taught courses are not new, of course, but generally consist of different persons teaching for, say, three weeks each, rather than each class consisting of sections taught by different people. Dividing a course into three or four self-contained segments might seem like an efficient way of doing things when education is defined as the transmission of information, but in terms of modelling patterns of nurture and community it has the distinct disadvantage of perpetuating the individualism that has caused so much damage within Western culture. In relation to theological education, our churches desperately need wholesome role models showing how people can work in partnership with one another, without being either threatened or threatening. In recent years I have often taught in partnership with my wife, and class members have consistently identified this as one of the most valuable aspects of the whole experience – seeing how women and men can work alongside one another as equal partners in the ministry of the church.

## Creating safe spaces

This should be a natural outcome of an interactive way of being, though it will only become so if the teachers are genuinely prepared to relinquish control and accept that they themselves are one resource among many within the group. A key element in this will, of course, be the temperamental disposition of the teacher, who must be able to be trusted to deal with absolutely anything that any-one might say, and not to make students feel stupid. Here again, though, I think that having sufficient time available for issues to be raised with the expectation that they might be adequately dealt with there and then will make a major contribution to the creation of an atmosphere in which students can say and ask absolutely anything at all, including honest statements about their own ignorance, as well as the unsatisfactoriness of some of my own responses. When teachers facilitate the creation of a genuinely safe space, a whole series of major benefits accrues to the students and to the educational process. I was genuinely amazed when I first began to experiment with this kind of model, and realized how much open sharing and mutual affirmation in the learning process it could generate. I am now regularly finding that both students and myself are being inspired to new levels of relationship, with one another and with the material being studied.

I have consistently found that people are enabled to share at a deeper level within this kind of context, including even quite shy people who might not normally take an active part in group dis-cussions. Indeed, I had a striking example of that the very first time

I used this method in a British university, of a young woman in her third year of a degree course but who told me that she had never spoken in any class whatever in the whole of her time as a student because her hearing was impaired. In this course, though, she eventually played a leading role, simply because the small-group work challenged her, on the one hand (she had to say something if she was with only one or two others), but on the other hand provided her with a safe space in which to work out what she might contribute, and how she might do it. From that base she ultimately felt confident enough to be able to move on and share openly and without embarrassment even within the larger group (which in that particular case was almost forty people). More recently, I have been teaching a course on the family using the same methodology, and I was amazed that within the first two class meetings a fifth of those present had volunteered their own stories of family dysfunction – some of them sharing experiences of abuse and violence quite openly with the entire class, while others confided in me or their closer student friends on a more personal basis. I also recall a class where one young woman arrived on a Monday morning to tell us that the day before she had been at what for her was an outstanding experience of community in a secular setting that she felt was more 'real' than what she experienced in church. The course had already been considering matters related to evangelism and the renewal of community life, and to one degree or another most others in the class empathized with what she said, though she did not elaborate on the nature of the occasion. This particular course was an intensive, meeting each day over a two-week period, and by the next day she was ready to say a bit more about her experience: on that Sunday, instead of going to church (which, she imagined, was what most seminary students ought to do!) she had joined her sister and her friends for a wedding at the beach. The following day, she returned again to her weekend experience, and told me right up-front with the entire class listening that, actually, it had been her sister's wedding – to another woman – and that she had found in that gay and lesbian community a greater sense of acceptance than she normally did in the church. She was not a lesbian herself, but still knew that she was taking a calculated risk, and that some members of the class would not necessarily be receptive to this news – but she had clearly discerned that overall this was a place of safety where she could explore theology in a context of personal journeying and spiritual growth. She was right – and if only we knew how to create such safe spaces in our churches, we might find ourselves able to engage more effectively with the spiritual searchers in today's world.

### Class members as an educational resource

One of the other things that is happening here is that the participants in the learning experience are themselves being valued as the major educational resource. This places more responsibility on students for their own learning, as well as creating new opportunities for more adventurous corporate exploration of the subject matter. Very often, a traditional lecture-based model can amount to little more than the teacher telling the students what they could easily read in books for themselves, and therefore actually provides a disincentive for students to engage with the material for themselves. By focusing class time on the task of doing something creative with what is in the books, and expecting students to take steps to familiarize themselves with reading materials, different educational possibilities are integrated from the start. Lest this might sound like a counsel of perfection, I hasten to add that I have found students engaged in this kind of holistic learning to be infinitely more highly motivated to read books than others who are being taught along more conventional lines. Perhaps there is less room to escape and mask one's ignorance in a group of people who come together as a community in this way, or maybe (as I would like to think) it is just so much more pleasurable an experience that students are prepared to put more effort into it, because there is a more immediately rewarding outcome. Either way, it has been interesting to me to observe that both commitment and attendance have consistently hit record levels in every class I have taught along these lines.

The other side of shifting more responsibility onto students to learn for themselves what is easily accessible through books and other resources is that teachers need to put some additional effort into making sure that those resources are clearly identified and easily available. A key element in this will be the provision of an extensive course handbook containing comprehensive reading lists as well as guidance on assignments, and a careful explanation of the rationale behind it all, so that students can fully understand what is going on. In the case of the course *Spirituality and Creativity for Evangelism and Worship*, this handbook runs to something like 150 pages, and in addition to the items mentioned includes resources for use in worship as well as instructions for group work and copies of diagrams, transparencies and so on that might be used in class.

In effect, the role of the teacher is to be a mentor and resource person rather than a lecturer in the narrow understanding of that word. The precise shape of the mentoring that might be required and appropriate will vary from one group of people to another, which is why it is also important to pay some attention to the actual learning needs of each unique group of students. I have regularly used the Honey and Mumford *Learning Styles Questionnaire* as an aid to this.[4] Working through it in the first class meeting of a course not only helps students relate to one another and begin to be aware of their own differences from others, but also gives the tutor invaluable insight into their learning needs. By linking that to reflection on the insights, experience and previous understandings that students are bringing to the topic, it is relatively easy then to construct future classes that will be tailor-made to fit the specific needs, interests and learning styles of those who are part of the group. This may sound like a risky enterprise, and of course in some ways it is, because once the teacher has asked questions of this sort, he or she must be prepared to do something to address them. But I think learning is like spirituality: a good teacher can help to define the infrastructure of learning, but what is then built upon that must always be a partnership between teacher and students.

### Spiritually enriching teaching and learning

Different institutional settings present their own opportunities and limitations. In the UK, theological education has to some extent been reduced to a subdepartment of the study of religion, which inevitably means that any reference to spiritual development becomes more or less problematic. Much of our teaching of

---

[4] Details of this can be found at http://www.psi-press.co.uk

theology takes place in the setting of universities, which often claim to be in the business of providing value-free education. They are not, of course, for no learning is value-free, and what has actually happened is that an educational system which in many cases was originally founded on Christian values has now espoused atheistic secular values instead. This is particularly the case in the humanities (where theology tends to be placed), though in business studies, social science, and medical education there does not seem to be the same evident embarrassment about talking of values. In some respects, the humanities are the last stronghold of modernity, for nowhere else in today's culture would it be assumed that atheism is to be identified with objectivity. Surprisingly, though, even in some theological colleges and seminaries much the same assumption prevails, and while worship, for instance, might find a place it is more likely to be defined by what happens in the chapel than integrated into what takes place in the classroom.

Spirituality is of course broader than worship – though we would do well to remember Martin Luther's dictum that 'work is worship', and be aware of the spiritual dimensions of the whole of life.[5] Spiritually formative education encompasses a lot more than structured worship. For example, when the teacher becomes a mentor to the students rather than merely a lecturer, that is itself a spiritually empowering way of teaching and learning. Being part of a community of learning is also itself a spiritually enriching experience. But I am convinced that, to achieve all the aims set out here, worship – defined as broadly or as narrowly as we will – should also be a central part of the learning experience itself, particularly through sensitive exploration of the tactile and the symbolic.

## Institutional Concerns

Much of what I have described could be put into operation by enterprising individuals, and indeed that might be the way to do it as institutions work out how to create experiences in theological

---

[5] Cf. Robert J. Banks, *Faith Goes to Work* (Bethesda, MD: Alban Institute, 1993); Matthew Fox, *Wrestling with the Prophets* (San Francisco: HarperSanFrancisco, 1995).

teaching and learning that will have integrity with their purposes and also equip people to minister effectively in today's culture. But there are some aspects of this that would require institutions to make structural and procedural adjustments in order to move from theory to practice. At least three areas are readily identifiable, and I want to mention two of them briefly, before dealing with the third at some length.

### The timetable

One very obvious area that would require some changes is in the way that time is used, for most colleges and seminaries organize things in blocks of 50–60 minutes. Rooms are made available on that basis, and assumptions are made about the likely commitments of individual students within that frame of reference. But integrated courses of the kind I have described cannot be taught in this way. On the basis of my experience, I would tend to go further, and say that not much that is worth knowing can be learned like that – though some subjects undoubtedly lend themselves to the traditional model better than others. I could not imagine Hebrew or Greek being taught in four-hour blocks, for example – though that might be due to my lack of imagination, and someone else might easily work out a creative and interactive way of doing it. Apart from the pedagogical reasons I have put forward here, there are also solid commercial considerations that would suggest institutions should take a serious look at this proposal. There are already growing numbers of people in theological education on a part-time basis, and if my analysis of emerging lifestyles is correct, that number is bound to increase, while the full-time residential student might well cease to exist altogether as a significant group. The colleges and seminaries that will recruit the most students in this changing marketplace will be those which offer the greatest flexibility. It is no use just allowing people to enrol on a part-time basis in classes that have been timetabled for the benefit of the full-time student, as that could mean an individual needing to be present for just one hour a day for four days of the week – a schedule that might technically amount to part-time study, but which would hardly make sense in even the most flexible of 'designer' lifestyles. But a course unit that meets for a full morning, afternoon or evening is a much more marketable commodity, and even people in full-time employment might be able to organize things in such a way that they can manage that. This is what it will mean for ministry to be integrated with life in a holistic balance.

## Space and accommodation

The actual location and design of the teaching and learning environment is another matter that needs to be addressed. The major difficulty in applying this model more widely would undoubtedly be the nature of the accommodation available in most institutions, whose buildings were never designed for this kind of operation. Lecture theatres are clearly impractical, but so are many other rooms. Those who calculate things like space requirements usually assume that people will be packed in as tightly as possible, and will sit in rows or round tables the whole time. Moreover, moving into small groups is not always easy, and activities such as role-play can be very difficult in some spaces simply because there is too much (or inappropriate) furniture. This highlights one of the major challenges in many institutions: at a time when for educational reasons we need to be innovative and creative, the physical body language of many buildings actually inhibits this, and effectively sets the educational agenda in an unhelpful way. Though theological students (and their teachers) can regularly be heard complaining of the reluctance of churches to move seats and other furniture to meet the needs of worshippers, the reality is that theological colleges and seminaries are far less likely to change the furniture than the average church – and when they do, they generally replace it with newer versions of what they already have. If, as I believe, more theological education will take place in the community, and not on seminary and college campuses, institutions will be likely to need less accommodation in the future, but what they do have will need to be of a quality to match what can be found elsewhere. Well-lit rooms with proper air conditioning, attractive carpeting and soft furnishings, the facility for making snacks and enough space for people to move around without being on top of one another will themselves say something about the nature of our enterprise and, ultimately, of the welcoming God whom we seek to serve.

## *Assessment*

Arguably, our educational systems overall are too obsessed with grades and not sufficiently concerned with the development of personal qualities that cannot easily be measured and quantified. This is particularly relevant in the context of theological education which aims to produce whole persons, rather than merely persons who happen to know a lot of information – and the more emphasis there is on personal maturity and somewhat intangible things like spirituality, the more we need to pay attention to the matter of assessment, and the development of appropriate criteria. It is clear to me that courses of the kind I am advocating here cannot easily be assessed through essays and written exams alone, though it is equally clear that they can be integrated into wider patterns of assessment in a way that does not need to be regarded as dumbing down the system. The need is for greater flexibility in methods of assessment, that will reflect the varied levels at which students learn.

Having monitored the outcomes of courses I have taught like this over the years, I have no hesitation in saying that, as well as fulfilling all the other educational and spiritual criteria set out here, the more innovative approach actually leads to a better learning experience when that is measured in terms of the final grades achieved by students. The students I am teaching now are consistently outperforming previous generations, and scoring higher grades than those who took courses with me on the same subjects, but who were taught and assessed more traditionally.

One of the central aspects of this has been the consistent use of a course journal as a core tool which can be used to help students to organize their learning, as well as forming a part of their assessed work (along with book reviews, essays or fieldwork studies, and an end-of-course exam if that is appropriate). There are no rigid guidelines for the writing of a journal, but students are given a general idea of how to go about it, by way of a checklist that includes aims and objectives of the class, what questions students had to start with, what has been learned, new questions that may have been stimulated, new tasks the student may identify, how it all relates to the student's personal learning goals – and what the student intends to do to address these matters. I usually establish only two fixed rules for the writing of a course journal. The first is that it should be honest, and it is OK for students to say how they feel, whether that is positive or negative; and the second is that it should amount to no more than a maximum of two A4 sides for each class meeting. This means in theory that a typical course journal might consist of maybe 18–20 sides for an entire semester or quarter, though in practice most of them write more. The grades given for completed journals are then based on the diligence with which the work has been thought through and carried out, rather than on the actual content *per se* (which may, for example, be critical of the tutor or the way particular topics were handled). Successful and mutually acceptable assessment of this kind of work obviously depends on a high degree of trust between students and tutor, which is why the learning environment and group dynamic is an important foundation on which to build this form of assessment – though with journals (as also with essays and project work) I regularly ask students to submit their own evaluation of their worth, highlighting their own strengths and weaknesses as they see them, and that in itself is a valuable learning experience with wider application as a life skill well beyond the narrow educational context.

Journalling has at least three very obvious advantages. First, students themselves have consistently highlighted the usefulness of this exercise, as it encourages them after each class to try to identify what exactly they have learned and what they need to do with that learning. In one sense it is encouraging them to do what the best students always have done, for it provides motivation to process material from each class at the time, rather than leaving it until later. Second, it has immeasurable benefits for the teacher, for the comments in course journals provide invaluable feedback on the learning process. Having a detailed breakdown of every single class is extremely useful and gives a clear picture of the value of everything that took place: what has worked, what has not worked and what might need to be changed in the future. No traditional end-of-course evaluation questionnaire could ever be as specific and detailed as a well-written set of journals. Third, a journal can be of considerable value to students who, for one reason or another, fail to complete other assignments (especially things like unavoidable absence from exams). For a course journal provides evidence of engagement with the work of the class and reflection on the topics covered. In the assessment of students studying science subjects, laboratory reports have always played such a role, but in subjects like theology it has often been more difficult to identify appropriate material. The course journal fits that requirement perfectly.

A similar approach can also be taken in respect of written assignments, allowing greater flexibility than is often the case, yet with greater challenge to the student's overall learning, because it also involves more responsibility. For example, I regularly offer students the option of writing either a regular essay-style paper, or undertaking some kind of fieldwork or case study. By encouraging students to choose their own subject matter and methodology, the actual process of researching and presenting a topic can then become totally transparent while also instilling its own sense of discipline and purpose into the exercise. It is actually a demanding thing to be invited to select a topic for investigation, especially when (as is invariably the case) students are required to present a formal proposal to be approved some time in advance of the submission date. A typical proposal might be expected to include not only a topic, question or other form of title, but a list of resources that are believed to be relevant to it, together with an indication of the methodology to be adopted in exploring it. In the case of practically oriented projects and fieldwork studies, it will be important to encourage self-critical reflection on the aims and objectives of the work in hand, so that they are not simply factual reports of what has taken place. The subsequent discussion of how to do this between teacher and student is itself a learning experience that not only tends to enhance the quality of the particular piece of work, but also helps students to understand how to establish models and procedures for any kind of research project, and thereby facilitates the development of transferable skills that can be invaluable in many aspects of future work and ministry – not to mention the less tangible (though no less valuable) benefits of this kind of mentoring in terms of knowing how to build relationships and work in partnership with other people.

## Getting There from Here

As I have already said, there will be more than one way to engage with the changing shape of ministry and the knock-on effect of that in the kind of theological education that might be appropriate for the new cultural paradigm. But whatever approach is adopted, it seems obvious to me that doing nothing is not an option. Nor can we afford the luxury of tinkering around with the peripherals first: we need rather to address the major questions of purpose and style. To succeed within the emerging marketplace, we may need to be ready for some radical thinking. In particular, we need to consider how to break out of the outmoded model of theological education that was inspired by the rationalist, materialist and reductionist perceptions of Enlightenment thinking, and start bringing things together across traditional disciplines, rather than fragmenting them. The way to do this may be through a thematic approach anchored in the practical needs of both students and churches, from which learning can network inductively into classical studies of scriptural texts, church history, and so on. If I was asked to categorize most of my own current teaching along the lines of traditional theological disciplines, I would hardly know where to begin. The course on *Spirituality and Creativity for Evangelism and Worship*, for instance, includes inductive approaches to biblical studies, as well as historical, philosophical and cultural analysis, missiology, creative arts (both theory and practice), worship and hermeneutics, alongside other aspects of personal spirituality. It is ostensibly concerned with a topic in practical theology, of course, but by being such it both transcends and incorporates the boundaries of many other traditionally discrete fields of theological enquiry. The same could be said of the course on *Theological and Pastoral Perspectives on the Contemporary Family*, which incorporates most of the subjects just mentioned, together with aspects of psychology, sociology and pastoral care. While my own starting point has been practical theology, I have no doubt that similarly inclusive courses could be taught beginning from any point on the spectrum of theological enquiry – indeed, I have on occasion done the same thing myself with courses on the New Testament. Though others will no doubt come up with different kinds of packages, I am certain that the sort of educational experience that will equip the church and its ministry to face the challenges of the twenty-first century will be based on something like the holistic principles I have outlined here. Only by engaging with this challenge will we be able to meet the need for integration between faith and life that those who are already in the church are demanding, and for which so many who are not as yet Christian are searching.

Chapter 8

# Making Theology Practical: Three Movies and the Contemporary Spiritual Search[1]

One of the most remarkable success stories of the final years of the twentieth century was the amazing resurgence of the movie industry. In the early 1980s, cinema audiences were falling all around the world, and it looked as if little could be done to change things. Today, Hollywood is riding the crest of a wave, making more money than ever before, and doing so not merely because of clever marketing strategies, but more especially because the films now being produced are addressing the major issues of life, death, and the survival of humanity and the planet that have come to dominate the emerging reflective spirituality of our time. Anyone wanting to know what questions people are now asking, and where they are searching for answers, need only look at the output of the movie industry. It was perhaps entirely predictable that, in a post-modern world that is characterized, among other things, by images, this was inevitably and naturally always going to be the case. For films not only reflect the popular mood – they also help to create it, so that even people who thought they had no profound questions about the meaning of all things find that they do when they visit the cinema to view the latest blockbuster.

Moreover, the constant search for ultimate meanings is so endemic within today's movies that it would be possible to dip at

[1] The annual Christ's College Lecture, delivered at the opening of the academic session in the University of Aberdeen, September 1998. In a slightly different form and under the title 'Racing Towards 2001: New Ways of Being for the Next Century' much of the same material was delivered as the Viking Lecture at the Royal College of Surgeons of Edinburgh (also in September 1998).

random into just about any selection of recent films and find there clues to the spiritual search of today's culture. To illustrate this, I have done exactly that, and the three movies I want to deal with here have been selected on the purely coincidental basis that they all happened to have been released in summer 1998. These are *The Truman Show*, *The X-Files* and *Armageddon*. Of the three, it was entirely predictable that two of them would become box-office successes, for even if they had had no storyline their special effects alone were bound to guarantee that there would be no shortage of eager viewers. But the third, *The Truman Show* – and the one I wish to begin with – came from nowhere, yet within a matter of days of its release, it was amazing audiences everywhere. It seemed like a certain B-movie, with goofy actor Jim Carrey apparently trying to be serious for the first time, but then against all the odds it became a transformational experience for those who saw it – not only for ordinary cinema-goers, but also for the professional reviewers. One critic described it as 'daring and original, a film that leaves you stunned and debating its message as the credits roll. I've never seen anything like it.'[2] Another wrote, 'Rarely, if ever, has a film proffered such a provocative premise as *The Truman Show*, much less risen to the challenge of exploiting it . . . a strange and wonderful fable that would seem destined for status as an immediate classic.'[3]

## Three Movies

### *The Truman Show*[4]

For the benefit of readers who may not have seen this film, let me give a brief synopsis of its story. *The Truman Show* is, as its name implies, a film about a film – or, rather, in this case, a film about a TV series. The opening words, spoken by a TV announcer at the start of

---

[2]  *Spliced* (July 1998).
[3]  *Box Office* (July 1998).
[4]  *The Truman Show*, directed by Peter Weir, written by Andrew Niccol, starring Jim Carrey as Truman Burbank, Laura Linney as Meryl, Ed Harris as Christof, Noah Emmerich as Marlon. Released by Paramount Pictures.

each programme in the series (but which we only hear for the first time midway through the film), provide a cryptic clue to the theme of the entire production:

> From the network that never sleeps – broadcasting live and unedited 24 hours a day, 7 days a week, around the globe . . . with Truman Burbank as himself, taped in the world's largest studio, one of only two man-made structures visible from space (the other being the Great Wall of China), comes the longest-running documentary soap opera in history, now in its thirtieth great year – *The Truman Show*.

Despite the larger-than-life character of the unctuous TV announcer, it still takes a while before one registers the precise significance of what is going on. But the key phrases are 'Truman Burbank as himself, taped in the world's largest studio . . . now in its thirtieth great year'. The show is in its thirtieth year, because Truman has just passed his twenty-ninth birthday. Conceived in obscurity, to parents we never hear of, Truman was adopted even before his birth by the OmniCam Corporation, and destined to become the star of a never-ending soap opera. The first episode featured his birth, live on TV, and since that moment literally everything he has done has been watched by a worldwide audience, captured by thousands of hidden miniaturized cameras. Truman is therefore the only 'real' person in this entire drama: apart from him, everyone else who has ever featured in his life – from the people who serve him in the shops, to the police officers who direct traffic in his street, to his wife Meryl and his best friend Marlon – all of them have been actors. His entire life has been a fiction, lived out in the artificial bubble of a TV studio that is located somewhere in the Hollywood Hills. From childhood to adulthood, every aspect of his existence has been contrived and planned according to the whim of Christof, the creator of the show.

    Truman, of course, has no idea that this is the case. For him, the small town of Seahaven, set on the coast of an idyllic subtropical island, is real. It is such a perfect environment that it has never really occurred to him to imagine that it might be worth going anywhere else – even though it would be just a short drive across a causeway linking it to the mainland. Why would anyone wish to leave a place where the sun always shines and everyone seems happy and contented with their life, and constantly friendly and cheerful? Besides, what Truman knows of the rest of the world does not encourage him to take much interest in it. From what he hears, it seems a harsh and dangerous place. Like everything else in Seahaven, however, the news bulletins are made to order by the show's director, so it is entirely predictable that the outside world should compare most unfavourably with the life he knows.

Truman's life itself has not been without its moments of pain and personal crisis. As a child, he remembers seeing his 'father' swept out to sea and drowned – an experience that instilled in him a fear of water, which itself served to discourage him from taking an interest in leisure pursuits such as sailing or swimming. But by the time we meet him, he has a settled job selling insurance, and is married to the lovely Meryl, with whom he is deeply in love. The job is fake, of course, and the people he thinks are his colleagues and clients are all actors. So is Meryl: like everyone else in Truman's life, she is a professional, hired by Christof to play a part. One of her major roles in the TV series is to make sure that the show's commercial sponsors receive their fair share of advertising, which means that she constantly speaks the language of a salesperson, drawing attention to the benefits of the domestic appliances and cleaning materials she uses, as well as the clothes she wears and the fast food she eats – all of which can be bought by viewers from the Truman mail-order cata-logue. Truman is blissfully unaware of all this and, since this is all he has ever known he assumes that everyone talks this way in their kitchen, bathroom, or even bedroom. But Meryl, like everyone else except Truman, is wearing a concealed earpiece through which Christof can give directions about what to say and do next while also maintaining the atmosphere of open-ended flexibility that is essential if Truman is really to be himself and react spontaneously to what is going on around him. There are a few potential flashpoints, as Christof insists that the next stage in the script requires Meryl to get pregnant, or when the truth begins to dawn on Truman and he gets angry with Meryl in ways that the script had not foreseen (and which therefore was not in her contract). But they are all dealt with in a totally detached, professional way, as Christof arranges for Truman to have a new romance with a work colleague called Vivian, with whom it is also intended he should have a child.

Up to the point where the film picks up Truman's story, though, there has only been one real problem for the show's owners and director, and that was during his teenage years, when a college dance went wrong and, instead of falling in love with Meryl as the script required, Truman became close friends with a girl called Lauren instead. Unlike the scripted version, this was true love, and Lauren managed to arrange a secret liaison at the beach one night, which went unnoticed even by Christof until the last moment. Her plan had been to tell Truman the truth about his life, but before she managed to do so someone claiming to be her father drove up and angrily insisted she return home with him. She never appears again, and Truman is told that she had moved to Fiji with her family – which explains why that is the only place outside Seahaven that he imagines he might wish to visit some day. In reality, of course, she was fired from the cast – and from time to time we see her in the outside world, watching the show on TV and willing Truman to discover its secrets.

Truman's fear of water, dating back to the fictitious drowning of his unreal father, together with the obvious benefits of life in Seahaven, have been sufficient to keep him where the OmniCam Corporation needs him to be. He has in effect become a prisoner, conditioned by his upbringing to have no ambitions to leave the island, and unwittingly controlled by a fascist director who cues everything from weather systems, to traffic jams, to sex, to marital conflict, in order to keep the story interesting for the viewers. With his every movement filmed at close quarters, he might as well be living in a cage. Then things begin to unravel. Even someone as naïve as Truman Burbank starts to suspect that something funny is going on. One day he sees a man in the street who bears a striking resemblance to his 'father'. He is, of course – but by now he too has left the cast and has broken into the set dressed as a hobo, though he is whisked away by security guards on a bus before his intentions become clear. Another day, a stage light unexpectedly falls from the clouds outside Truman's house. Driving his car, he turns the radio on, only to hear what the audience knows are stage directions for the actors in his own life – though Christof jams the signals as soon as he realizes what is happening. Eventually, Truman decides to drive off the island over the causeway that links it to the mainland, just to see what is at the other side. Within seconds, traffic jams appear from nowhere, and a nuclear alert sounds from a nearby facility, closing down the entire highway system. It takes a while for him even to begin to imagine that everyone in his world might be conspiring against him, for from his perspective they are all his friends.

But eventually, he determines to leave the island to see once and for all what might be beyond it. Escape by sea is the last remaining practical option, and he takes to the water in a small sailing boat. Of course, that leaves him vulnerable not only to his own fears, but also to all the special effects that Christof can throw at him. And he does – until eventually, the production team have to decide whether Truman is more valuable to them dead or alive. Christof toys with the possibility of killing him – musing that, since he was born on a TV show, it would be entirely natural for him to die on one – but eventually the only way forward seems to be for Christof to speak directly to him, to reveal the truth, and hope that Truman will stay nevertheless. But to no avail: Truman crosses the sea, reaches the edge of the set, finds a door in the horizon (which, after all, is only a painted backdrop), and goes through it in search of the other world beyond Seahaven.

### The X-Files[5]

From a dramatic and artistic perspective, the second film – *The X-Files* – is simply not in the same league as *The Truman Show*. Like the TV series on which it is based, this movie has only a very tenuous storyline running through it. Instead, what we have are a series of unresolved questions and innuendoes about the meaning of life, all interspersed with more or less unbelievable scenes in which Mulder and Scully run along lots of dark alleyways, examine horribly disfigured dead bodies, and survive death-defying incidents that range from being stung by bees to Scully all but having the life sucked out of her by alien viruses deep beneath the ice of the Antarctic. But its underlying questions are remarkably similar to those raised in *Truman* – not least of which are its preoccupation with how we might tell the difference between what is real and what is make-believe.

---

[5]  *The X-Files*, directed by Rob Bowman, written by Chris Carter, starring David Duchovny as Fox Mulder and Gillian Anderson as Dana Scully.

There is, of course, enough of a story to give it credibility. The opening scene is set in 35,000 BC and shows a couple of prehistoric people being attacked by a mysterious black gooey substance which kills them and consumes their organs, before retreating into some kind of suspended animation, where it remains until its reappearance in modern times in what has by now become north Texas. The same stuff, still living just below the ground alongside a new housing development, kills a child, as well as some firefighters who enter an underground cave to try to rescue him. All along, the existence of this toxic substance – later identified as a primeval virus, and the original inhabitant of the planet – has been known to the authorities, who are then forced into a cover-up which leads to a plan to destroy the evidence of the bodies by having them blown up in what is made to look like a 'terrorist' bombing of a government building in downtown Dallas. Before long, however, Mulder and Scully have tracked down the remains, and Scully's medical knowledge has allowed her to identify the extraterrestrial nature of the black-goo virus. When Mulder coincidentally meets an old friend of his father's, the truth about the explosion becomes clear, and other more sinister events come into focus, involving plagues, viruses, global conspiracies and alternative governments waiting in the wings to seize power. It is only a matter of time before Mulder and Scully have uncovered a breeding facility for the virus, and traced its origins back to alien spacecraft deep beneath the Antarctic, whose presence is being kept a closely guarded secret by conspirators who eventually capture Scully and entomb her in their icy fortress. Mulder – as always – acts on his intuitions and against all the odds discovers her location, from which he manages to rescue her at the last minute.

### *Armageddon*[6]

The notion that there is some malevolent force out there ready to strike fear into the hearts of us all becomes the central focus – indeed, the only *raison d'être* – of *Armageddon*. There can be little doubt that the main virtue of this movie lies in the sheer noise and

---

[6] *Armageddon*, directed by Michael Bay, written by Jonathan Hensleigh and J. J. Abrams, starring Bruce Willis as Harry S. Stamper, Billy Bob Thornton as Dan Truman, Ben Affleck as A. J. Frost, Liv Tyler as Grace Stamper, Will Patton as Chick Chapple. Released by Buena Vista Pictures.

spectacle of its special effects, as rocks, planets, spacecraft and nuclear devices jostle for position to try, variously, to bring about the end of the world, or to prevent it from happening. Even the special effects become tedious and repetitive after a while, and while watching it I had the distinct feeling that I may have been viewing the same sequences over and over again. It is so banal that it has even been compared unfavourably with *Independence Day*, on the basis that that at least made some attempt at reflection on how people might perhaps come to terms with the impending extinction of their planet.

Still, there is a storyline here, even though it is almost totally unbelievable, and is expounded in dialogue that is, at best, basic and arbitrary. In brief, a giant asteroid is on a collision course with the earth, and unless it can be either destroyed or diverted, there is only one possible outcome: life as we know it will be exterminated. As the best scientific brains get to work on the problem, they soon realize there is no obvious rational solution. The best they can do is to think laterally, imagine the unimaginable – and hope that it may work. The unimaginable turns out to be a plan to detonate a nuclear device deep beneath the asteroid's surface, in an effort to blow it apart, and working out how to accomplish this then occupies the remainder of the film. On the one hand some of the technology exists – in the form of the NASA space shuttle – but on the other hand, no one has the slightest idea how to bring the plan together. The unlikely resolution of this problem comes in the form of a collection of social misfits, whose only employment hitherto has been in oil exploration. The theory is that they know how to drill holes, so they can be sent to the asteroid, then drill a hole 800 feet deep, right through to its centre, in which the nuclear device can be exploded, thereby splitting the giant rock (the size of Texas) in such a way that its two halves will pass either side of the earth.

The reality, of course, is not quite that simple. But after many trials and tribulations, and much noise and visual special effects, the task is accomplished and the earth and its people are saved.

## Searching for New Ways

As I said at the start, these films were chosen at random, and maybe the most obvious thing that they have in common is that they were all released in 1998. But precisely because of the randomness of their choice, and the very different styles and quality that they display, the similarities of their themes are all the more striking, and lead me to suggest that they are reflecting some key issues for our culture. Moreover, they are key theological issues.

## The nature of reality

What is real, and how can we be sure? *The Truman Show* raises this in a particularly brilliant way. What Truman *thinks* is real is completely artificial – and everyone in the entire world knows that, except for him. As he works through his own personal identity questions, Truman draws our attention to one of the most fundamental questions of human existence: How do we think we know what we know? Or, to put it another way, where is truth to be found? Or, even more profoundly, is there such a thing as truth anyway – and if there is, how might we recognize it? Those of course are the central ontological and epistemological questions of all time. While there have been many nuances in the ways they have been addressed over the centuries, until relatively recently Western thinkers would have had a fairly consistent answer to them, and would certainly have been agreed that the way to find an answer must be through the exercise of autonomous human reason. Descartes' Latin dictum *Cogito ergo sum* (I am thinking therefore I am) would certainly have been lurking in the background, if not explicitly invoked, and it would have been taken for granted that, while rationality and its companions materialism and reductionism may not be perfect, they could certainly be trusted to point us in the right direction.

As we have seen already, that vision, rooted in the optimistic worldview of the European Enlightenment, and beyond that in the rationality of Greek culture and philosophy, is now being rejected in a big way. It is widely believed that the present crisis in Western civilization is entirely the product of the application of this kind of thinking, and that many of the problems of our culture can be traced back to our love affair with rationality. It is argued that while the mechanistic, rationalist, reductionist worldview may have been an essential prerequisite for the emergence of the West as we know it – as a patriarchal, colonialist and dualistic socio-political entity – an unhealthy preoccupation with such things has led to the marginalization of human and spiritual values – and in any case, it was based on a lie, for perceptions of anything (reality included) depend on where the observer is looking from. Not only has this led to dysfunction within the environment, but it has also affected every aspect of human life, including forms of social organization. For it was rationalization, with its inbuilt need to categorize and classify things, that allowed us to create the categories that have led to some of the most profound divisions in our world: notions of difference between the races, between women and men, between people and animals and, ultimately, between people and their natural environment. To resolve the present crisis, that trend will need to be reversed.

As an essentially cognitive discipline, theology is still struggling to appreciate the extent to which the rejection of reason is now embedded in the communal psyche of the West – yet in all three of these films the rejection of rationality is the one thing that leads to a successful outcome.

One of the most frightening things about *The Truman Show*'s Seahaven is not that it is dark and unpredictable, but that it is exactly the opposite: it is totally rational, a perfect place where every home looks as if it was completed yesterday, and everyone appears to have a settled and satisfying life. In that sense, it is the ultimate expression of the rationalization of culture that began with industrialization, and is now manifesting itself as 'the McDonaldization of society'.[7] In this view of the perfect world, there is a place for everything, and everything knows its place. This is how life is when reason is projected into cultural reality. So we are not surprised that the possibility of escape for Truman Burbank only begins when he suspends his own reason and learns to trust his intuitions instead. Not only that, but in order to get out of his bubble, he actually acts contrary to the dictates of reason – for who would imagine that the moon is really the control room of a TV programme, or that the sky has a door in it that leads to another world?

Exactly the same theme surfaces in *The X-Files*. It is only because Mulder trusts his hunches that Scully is eventually released from her icy grave in the Antarctic. Had he gone with his reason, she would not have survived. There are clear points of contact here with

---

[7] Ritzer, *The McDonaldization of Society*.

aspects of the New Age worldview that were explored in an earlier chapter – indeed the entire movie is a good illustration of the practical outworking of Shirley Maclaine's claim that 'it all seems to be about "feeling", not thinking'.[8] *The X-Files* depict the forces of reason and rationalization locked in combat with hunches, intuitions and, in this case, the intervention of beings from other worlds – and, as with Truman, the way to achieve a successful outcome is through the suspension, if not the rejection, of rationality. On the one hand are the FBI and the powers of government as we know them. On the other is Fox Mulder, for whom the less rational a thing is, the more believable it seems to be. Somewhere in between is Dana Scully, who never quite knows which side to be on. This unlikely pair appeal to audiences precisely because, between them, they reflect the dilemma in which just about everybody finds themselves caught up. Scully is the quintessential product of the Enlightenment worldview, scientifically trained (she is a medic) and, therefore, sceptical of the possibility of anything non-rational, whether it be extraterrestrial life or, indeed, her own emotions (one of the big questions about the film before its release was whether she would eventually get around to kissing Mulder: she didn't). Mulder is different. His sister was abducted by aliens when he was a small child, and he believes in absolutely everything. At the same time, though, he also shows a healthy respect for Scully's scientific knowledge. But despite their differences, both of them distrust the Establishment.

The same theme surfaces again in *Armageddon*. Here, one might cynically say that the audience has to suspend their rationality in order to enjoy the film at all. From a logical perspective, the whole thing is meaninglessness – but in the end, it seems to make little difference that the special effects are repetitive, or that the plot is totally impossible to imagine and is overloaded with inconsistencies even within its own frame of reference. For here again, a major underlying theme is that, if there is a way of saving the planet, it is unlikely to be based on the normal rules of reason and rationality as we have understood them. The real struggle throughout the film is not so much between a threatened earth and a menacing asteroid, as between the scientific rationality of NASA and, behind it, the

---

[8]  Maclaine, *Out on a Limb*, 215.

Pentagon and its military advisers, and the totally illogical, though ultimately successful, strategy of the roughnecks. They do all the wrong things – getting drunk, even arrested, the night before their mission, and accidentally destroying a Russian space station which was vital for their supply line. But once they are on the uncharted asteroid, it is only Rockhound (who is one of the weirder personalities even among this strange bunch, and said to be suffering from 'space dementia') who knows exactly where they are – while the boffins at the Pentagon are completely in the dark about what is going on.

All this raises some profound questions for theology. The one thing that is certain is that the way we now seek to define and understand reality is no longer what it used to be. Whatever it may be called (post-modernity or whatever), a significant paradigm shift has taken place, and people are now looking for guidance in the most unlikely of places. Even in Britain, with its generally conservative culture, there are now more 'complementary' health practitioners than there are general practitioners of scientific medicine, and much of what is now happening would have seemed wacky and incredible only a generation ago. One might be forgiven for wondering if Western culture is not in danger of being over-taken by a great wave of irrationalism – something that we will return to in our next and final chapter.

But Truman raises another question, for as he escapes from his artificial bubble, I cannot help wondering on which side of the door real 'reality' is going to be found? If it seems impossible that anyone could live that way, then remember Princess Diana, who effectively existed in such a bubble from the day she was engaged to Prince Charles to the day she died. Moreover, our evidently insatiable fascination with so-called 'reality' TV shows, ranging from behind-the-scenes life of hospital wards, veterinary surgeries, airports, and other everyday locations – not to mention chat shows in which people reveal intimate details of their personal lives – raise similar questions. Indeed, some of the chat shows in particular really do make it look as if fiction might easily be more 'real' than truth. But similar questions are concerning us well beyond the world of the popular media, for example in relation to cloning, and the extent to which it is justifiable for people's lives to be engineered for them, even if such engineering might seem to be an improvement.

## *Our love-hate affair with technology*

At the same time as we are facing a massive questioning of
rationality, we continue to have an unresolved love-hate
relationship with the products of rationalization, especially in the
areas of science and technology. Most viewers would probably be
surprised to learn that Truman's Seahaven is actually a real place.
What we see on the screen is not some surrealist creation built on a
back-lot in Burbank, but the community of Seaside, in north-west
Florida. Dennis Gassner, production designer for *The Truman Show*,
describes it as follows:

> Built along a beautiful stretch of beach property in northwest Florida,
> Seaside is a 90-acre planned community founded by developer Robert
> Davis and his wife, Daryl, in 1980. Comprised of over 300 cottages
> used by year-round residents and vacation guests, Seaside features its
> own local post office, art galleries, antique shops, boutiques, book-
> stores and restaurants, all within walking distance of each home. The
> residents of Seaside conform to a unique building code, wherein each
> cottage is required to adhere to a neo-Victorian style of architecture –
> no ranch houses, no Colonials, no split-levels. Every home features a
> white picket fence, but no two fences on the same street are alike. And
> each of Seaside's streets lead to the ocean. The storybook cottages,
> which are all painted in cheery pastels, carry individual names, such as
> Eversong and Ain't Misbehaving, and feature porches, ample win-
> dows, and wide eaves . . . the visuals of the film's Seahaven really came
> from this community. It is a highly architecturally designed environ-
> ment – a kind of neoclassical, postmodern retro world, and quite
> unique.[9]

One of the contradictions of life today is that, while we are
apparently happy to question the technology which has made us
what we are, we are not prepared to discard it. In everyday life, this
might manifest itself in a resistance to using public transport instead
of cars, even though we know that exhaust emissions damage the
environment – or a mistrust of the work of the medical profession,
even though we know large numbers of us would not now be alive

---

[9]  On *The Truman Show* website: http://www.trumanshow.com

without its procedures. *The X-Files* and *Armageddon* both make this balancing act an explicit part of their story. While Mulder continually operates on his hunches, it is Scully's medical knowledge that allows them to be certain the Dallas bombing was neither an accident nor a terrorist plot; and in *Armageddon*, while there is a clear contrast between the rationality of NASA and the irrationality of the team, they still need the rational technology to enable them to get to their asteroid destination.

## Redefining our Values

In the midst of such a massive realignment of traditional understandings, it is not surprising that our value systems are also undergoing redefinition. This surfaces in these movies in a particular way that has relevance to our self-understanding, and ultimately raises significant moral questions.

### Who is in control of things? And does anybody care?

*The Truman Show*'s answer to the first is quite clear: Christof is the director. From his bank of TV monitors concealed within the moon, he serves a similar purpose to the clandestine and semi-criminal government-in-waiting of *The X-Files*, though there is always the underlying theme there implying that, in reality, dark and unknowable forces have the upper hand (aliens, the virus, etc.). *Armageddon* likewise has an open-ended answer, though with more than a hint that, in all probability, no one at all is in control and the universe is merely the product of random forces. The inclusion of such diverse possibilities simply reflects the diversity of views that would be held within the general population today.

More striking is the way that the majority of ordinary people seem not to care about ultimate meanings, preferring instead to focus on their own immediate concerns. Though the worldwide audience watching *The Truman Show* on TV expresses delight when he finally makes it across the sea and through the set door to the other side of the sky, the fact is that they have been uninterested in Truman's plight for the preceding thirty years. Just as long as the soap opera continued to bring them 24-hour-a-day entertainment, so they could tune in whenever they felt like it, no one seems to have cared. Indeed, the only substantive reason that Christof can think of to try to persuade Truman to stay is the claim that the show brings 'inspiration and hope to millions of people'. There is a scene in *Armageddon*, where two Japanese tourists are in a New York taxi when boulders from the sky begin falling on Manhattan, mysteriously exploding on impact and generally wreaking havoc all over the place. The entire street has just been transformed into a flaming wasteland, but the woman turns to her companion and complains, 'I want to go shopping'. Immediate needs take precedence even over life and death!

Truman's desire to go to Fiji falls into the same category. It is the kind of thing that people trapped in small-town lives say all the time – which is one reason why we know that he will never really go. He is typical of the way many people feel today, for he is trapped as much by his own inner fears as he is by his surroundings. In his case, he is quite literally trapped in his own life. No doubt this explains why it is widely supposed today that, if our lives are to be worthwhile and have meaning, then the only way that will happen will be as we take responsibility for ourselves. The Establishment cannot be trusted: experts – including especially theologians and other religious people – are seen as, at best, self-serving, at worst as conspiring against the rest of humanity.

### Taking responsibility for ourselves

We saw a striking example of people taking responsibility for themselves in the responses to the death of Princess Diana, which had very strong overtones of all these concerns which then combined to produce a sort of alternative spirituality that seemed to address the needs of people more effectively than the traditional answers of the Western religious tradition.

One of the features of today's world is the emergence of increasing numbers of 'designer' faiths, taking elements from traditional spirituality, both East and West, and mixing them with other secular belief systems so as to create a worldview that will address the personal insecurities felt so strongly by so many. The extraordinary diversity of the ingredients that might be used in such an enterprise is well illustrated in *The X-Files* – the TV series as well as the movie. Moreover, both *The Truman Show* and *Armageddon* have subtle references to aspects of the Christian tradition, though in each case a different spin is put on them, highlighting the way in which the emerging culture is prepared to adopt and use motifs from long-established traditions, while also freely changing them to suit its own underlying nostrums.

In *Truman*, the theme of good and evil focuses on Christof: is he God or is he the Devil? One of the most dramatic moments of the entire film is when Truman, nearly dead as a result of a fierce storm as he tries to cross the sea, is addressed by a voice from the sky which tells him, 'I am the Creator', and then after a pause continues, 'of a television show'. The parallel with the Judaeo-Christian God can hardly be unintended, as is also the case when Christof relates how he has watched Truman's every move, from birth to this moment onwards (his first smile, first steps, the loss of his first tooth, his first day at school and so on) – in words that clearly echo both the language and concepts of Hosea 11:3–4. At the same time, Christof is an evil, manipulating presence, who is ultimately prepared to kill the star of his show if watching him die will boost the ratings, and who is only restrained by his own chief executives – though it is not clear that they are operating from a moral basis, rather than a difference of opinion over marketing strategy. At those moments he is clearly behaving like the Devil. In the emerging paradigm, he can be both at once, of course. It is tempting to see here not only a reflection of the widely held New Age belief that good and evil are two sides of the same coin, but also a deliberate reversal of the Garden of Eden story, with Christof as an overpossessive patriarchal God and Truman as a naïve Adam, wanting to get out of Paradise because at least life might be more interesting somewhere else. Maybe he actually needs to sin before he can become a real person! Ultimately, it makes little difference how Christof is described: he can be both God and Devil at once. When taken to its logical conclusion and (as it often is) combined with a monistic worldview, that means there is neither good nor evil, only personal choices. This position is not actually commended in *The Truman Show*, but it is certainly one of the streams of thought running not far beneath the surface. In the culture at large, it is increasingly assumed that we have all chosen to be who we are – a process often described as choosing one's own karma. We have already mentioned this tendency, and highlighted some of its dangers, in the first chapter of this book. Ziauddin Sardar might be cynical when he observes that 'It's a genuine miracle that, given the western history of oppression and domination, the white man's karma always puts him on top'[10] – but he is certainly articulating a major ethical problem posed by this worldview. We never quite find out whether Truman is somehow being blamed for his initial predicament, though there is no question that he will only ever escape when he is prepared to take personal responsibility for his own life. But the other characters are all effectively in the same situation. Christof actually owns everyone, not just Truman – though the others definitely are willing collaborators, presumably because of the job security it gives them. This in turn raises other questions about what people will do for money: Meryl, playing Truman's wife, is quite happy to have an intimate relationship whose every detail is revealed through hidden TV cameras, and is clearly prepared to become pregnant, even though she never does. This is one key aspect of the post-modern spiritual search with which Christians have barely begun to come to grips. For while modernity can undoubtedly be criticized for the way it made possible untold mechanized suffering, it also had a moral conscience that could challenge it and, on occasions, call a halt. Post-modernity, however, places personal choice above everything else, and in the process not only makes community all but impossible to achieve, but also easily regards barbarism as just one lifestyle choice among others. In the process, it embraces evil by making values irrelevant – and so, Christof debates whether Truman should be allowed to live or die not on moral grounds, but purely in relation to the likely responses of the audience and, therefore, of the ratings and income of his show.

The nature and source of salvation itself also runs like a thread through the fabric of these movies. One of the few truly creative aspects of *Armageddon* is the way in which it deals with the question of how people might handle universal tragedy. Many reviewers complained about the focus on apparently illiterate heroes whose only skill was in detonating explosions. But therein

---

[10]  Ziauddin Sardar, *Postmodernism and the Other* (London: Pluto, 1998), 260.

lies one of its more sophisticated points, as it is suggested that the marginalized can become the saviours. Here too, however, there is a subtle rewriting of a bit of the Christian tradition. For instead of the nasty patriarchal God cruelly sacrificing his own son, Harry S. Stamper, the team leader, voluntarily offers himself as the sacrifice in order that his future son-in-law might live and be one of those who will create the next generation. It goes without saying, of course, that the saviours were all men! But there is a further limitation in the film's perception of who the saviours might be. As the film depicts scenes of the world's population in different countries, waiting to see if this really is the end, they all know that their future is totally dependent on the achievements of just one nation: the USA, which is however in effect a symbol for the whole of Western culture.

The days of Christendom and colonialism might be past, but post-modernity here emerges as a form of globalization that is merely the latest extension of the Western consciousness. The same theme underlies *The X-Files*, with its apparent endorsement of the insights of other cultures in seeking to understand the workings of the cosmos – though such wisdom is firmly controlled by the underlying values of Western culture. We have come across this attitude repeatedly in previous chapters as we have reviewed some of the ways in which Western people are trying now to reimagine the world using whatever materials may lie to hand. Today's culture has rightly been described as a spiritual supermarket, with 'products' taken from all and every culture, apparently implying that non-Western traditions can chart a new way forward. But what then happens to the spiritual goodies once they have been extrapolated from their original context shows that what is taking place is actually the exact opposite of that. Far from being an affirmation of the value of other cultures and their spiritualities, this process is actually the end of all cultures and spiritualities, insidiously sacrificed on the altar of globalization, which is of course Westernization. It might appear that the insights of other cultures are being taken seriously, as the role of traditional Western understanding is downgraded and elements of other ethnic origins are given a place in the new worldview that is emerging. But in reality, that is only happening because the questioning of rational categories has led to the conclusion that nothing is of any intrinsic value anyway, apart from its capacity for feeding the rapacious consumerism and individualism of Western culture. Post-modernity might present itself as the epitome of freedom, a way of deconstructing all hierarchy and control, and therefore dispelling domination and oppression. But its attitude to reality is, in fact, a reinvented form of totalitarianism. At one level it promotes itself as bringing an end to the hierarchy of truth established under colonialism and expanded by modernity, but at the same time it is creating its own monopoly of manufactured 'truth' through which control can still effectively be exercised.

## Looking Forward

If theology is to become and remain practical, these are some of the issues with which we need to engage. It has never been easy to answer the oldest question in the world – What is truth? – but it was probably a good deal easier to handle that than today's question, which is – Who cares anyway? One thing is certain, and that is that none of us can avoid being implicated in the search for relevant new ways of being that will characterize life in the new millennium. But it is unlikely to be a painless process. *Armageddon* is not an inappropriate image for what is already happening in terms of the disintegration of the culture our parents and grandparents knew. No one can predict what the new paradigm will eventually look like, for the questions now being raised are basic to any understanding of life and its meaning.

I think we are back to what is called 'square one'. We may timidly admit that we live in 'apostolic times', in times when the cloth is being woven. A risky time in apostolic mission, where we have to tell one another the basis of our hope, join with each other in the expression of the strength of our faith, telling one another the questions we have in order to find together the answers, that the world, the people, are expecting from us as disciples of Christ.[11]

---

[11]   Gert Rüppell, *Ecumenical Letter on Evangelism* (Geneva: WCC, December 1995), 6.

To meet this challenge, we will need to be more open than we have usually been, both about our own motivations and our own visions. In this circumstance, perhaps the most useful sense in which theology can be practical will be in creating safe spaces within which we can explore our own weakness and vulnerability, and rediscover our own spirituality and creativity as we engage in the important task of reimagining not just theology, but the world.

# Chapter 9

# What Is Worth Believing at the Beginning of the New Century?[1]

## A Spiritual Surprise

A few years ago I was invited to give an address during a mission in one of Britain's most ancient universities. My subject was 'Is the New Age compatible with Christianity?' There must have been something like four hundred people present, a good mixture of both professors and students. At the end of my talk, the person chairing the meeting asked for questions, and immediately drew a response – from a member of the university staff, who stood up and said, 'I am a professor of chemical engineering, and for the last fifteen years I have been a wizard. I would like to become a Christian.' To say that the chairperson was lost for words would be an understatement. He – together with most of the other Christians present – had no idea what to do next. In one sense, of course, this was precisely the kind of response they were hoping for. But at another level, it was a response they were ill-equipped to handle. For myself, I found it hard to decide which was the more surprising: that this educated man in his mid-forties might actually be what he claimed, or that he had the nerve to stand up in front of his common-room colleagues and make such a statement. Barely credible it might have been – but it was all true, as the college chaplain and I discovered when we visited his

[1] A Sermon preached in King's College Chapel, Aberdeen on Sunday 10 March 1996 at the annual service of the Convener Court of the Seven Incorporated Trades of Aberdeen. The Bible lessons were Exodus 3:1–6 and Mark 12:28–34. It is included here unchanged.

apartment later that same day. In conversation after the meeting, the professor suggested to me that 'If I'm to follow Jesus, I have a lot of stuff that needs to be dealt with.' As I walked toward his apartment, my mind was working overtime trying to imagine what this 'stuff' might be. As he opened the door, it became obvious what he was talking about, for the first thing we encountered was a witch's broomstick that fell from behind the door as it was pushed back. His desk was covered not with scientific manuals, but with books of magic spells, not to mention various magic feathers, magic bones and other implements the purpose of which I could scarcely begin to describe – while in another corner of the room was a bubbling pot full of brightly coloured liquid. He may have been a professor of a modern applied science, but this man was living like a medieval alchemist – and, yes, in the midst of it all he did seriously want to become a Christian. Though he did not realize it at the time (for his knowledge of the Bible was non-existent), what he spontaneously decided to do next recreated a scene taken straight out of the New Testament (Acts 19:19), as he removed all this magical equipment from his room and set fire to it in the centre of an ancient quadrangle.

## Culture in Crisis

It will surprise no one to hear that I have reflected many times on that experience. Like most people, I initially found the idea of a science professor who was a wizard, and who wanted to become a Christian, quite literally mind-blowing. Then I recalled how the nineteenth-century philosopher Friedrich Nietzsche had traced the development of what he perceived to be three stages of religious thought. As he surveyed the grand sweep of history, he claimed that in the earliest times human beings sacrificed one another to the gods. Later, they sacrificed their instincts, their nature, to the gods – and in the third and final stage, he said, they sacrificed God. After this sacrifice, he observed, there would be nothing left to worship but 'stone, stupidity, gravity, fate'. It is worth bearing in mind that when Nietzsche spoke of 'the death of God', he meant the disintegration of the entire religio-philosophical basis upon which Western civilization had been built. The 'death of God', in his words, was the death of the West. In his time, he could only observe that it was 'reserved for the generation which is even now arising'.[2] But today, we are that generation, and the 'death of God' in this sense is an inescapable part of our everyday experience. The whole framework of Western culture, going back through the Enlightenment and ultimately to the values of ancient Greek philosophy, is collapsing. And the experience is one of dislocation, scattering and insecurity. In the words of Yeats:

> Turning and turning in the widening gyre
> The falcon cannot hear the falconer;
> Things fall apart; the centre cannot hold;
> Mere anarchy is loosed upon the world . . .

Yet in the same poem, Yeats went on to affirm that disintegration is but the opportunity for the birth and emergence of a new order. His poem ends with this question:

> And what rough beast, its hour come round at last,
> Slouches towards Bethlehem to be born?[3]

There can be no doubt that we are in the midst of a paradigm shift of massive proportions – and one that will prove to be as significant as those which took place in the time of Galileo or Newton. Few people would deny that – and no one knows it better than the representatives of the traditional world of work. For many of the crafts which we come here today to celebrate are only marginally relevant to today's world, and the traditional values of ancient trades guilds are increasingly being displaced and pushed to the fringes of our culture. Moreover, not many people today are as optimistic as Yeats was as he surveyed the approaching cultural storm. We face many big questions – not least, How can we make sense out of what is going on? But above all, perhaps, What are the things that will be worth believing in the twenty-first century?

---

[2] For Nietzsche's three stages of religion, see his *Beyond Good and Evil*, paragraph 55; quoted here from the edition by R J Hollingdale (London: Penguin, 1973), 63.
[3] W. B. Yeats, *The Second Coming* (1921).

A major contender on the scene is the whole phenomenon of the so-called 'New Age' – a vast and amorphous collection of practices and beliefs of a vaguely 'spiritual' kind, ranging from a renewed interest in witchcraft and the paranormal, to a search for new holistic scientific models. As I survey the scene that is today's Western culture – intellectual culture as well as popular culture – Nietzsche's analysis seems more and more realistic. We are indeed worshipping at the altars of stone, stupidity, gravity and fate. One of the reasons for this, of course, is that the traditional Western source of spiritual wisdom (the church) seems to have dried up. For many people (and often with good reason), Christianity – at least as we have known it in the West – is part of the problem. So how can it possibly be part of the answer to the problem?

## Reimagining the Church

In this context, we may well ask what it might mean to be a Christian. Is it any longer worth following Jesus Christ? True, Western Christianity does seem to be powerless and too often bereft of spiritual reality – but for huge numbers of people elsewhere in the world, the answer to that question is beyond doubt. A recent survey of church life in Scotland shows that every week for the last ten years, something like 230 people have left the church – the equivalent of a good-sized congregation disappearing every seven days.[4] Yet according to David Barrett, editor of the *World Christian Encyclopedia*, in Africa alone 17,000 people become Christians every single day. In fact, the majority of all the Christians in the world are now non-white and non-Western people.[5] The whole centre of gravity of world Christianity has shifted dramatically in recent years, from the West to the two-thirds world. If Christianity is to have any relevance to the life of Western people in

---

[4] Peter Brierley (ed.), *Prospects for Scotland 2000* (London: Christian Research Association, 1995); cf. also Peter Brierley (ed.), *Religious Trends 1998/99*, No. 1 (London: Christian Research, 1998).
[5] David Barrett's major work is the *World Christian Encyclopedia* (New York: Oxford University Press, 1982); regularly updated in the first issue each year of *International Bulletin of Missionary Research*.

the twenty-first century, we will need to be ready to learn from the fast-growing churches of the rest of the world. Many of us will find it difficult to learn anything from them, because of our own imperialist past and the ingrained assumption that the rest of the world needs what we have, rather than the other way round. Nor should we underestimate the degree to which much of what is happening in the world church will threaten who we are and how we articulate our spirituality. But set alongside what looks like terminal decline in the Scottish churches (and statistically, there could be no Christians left in Scotland by about 2030), we have no alternatives but to seek new ways of following Christ. What then might we need to learn?

### Thinking and feeling

We have become excessively bookish, rational and cerebral in our faith. There is nothing wrong with thinking – quite the reverse, in fact, for rationality is one of the key hallmarks of being human. But in recent centuries we have developed a way of Christian believing that is concerned only with thinking. This has merely reflected the values of modern Western culture, which has tended to value the gifts of thinking much more highly than the gifts of feeling and doing – as a consequence of which, craftspeople have often found their creative manual labour downgraded as compared with the endeavours of those who are thinkers. Of course, we need a holistic balance – and today's lesson from Mark 12 depicts Jesus insisting as much, with his talk (following the Old Testament book of Deuteronomy) of loving God with one's heart, soul and strength – as well as the mind. But Matthew Fox puts his finger on much that is wrong with Western Christianity when he writes:

> So much of religion in over-developed countries is in books, academic institutions, degrees, sermons, and words. While learning is certainly essential to healthy religion, it is no substitute for praxis. Thinking about God is no substitute for tasting God, and talking about God is no substitute for giving people ways of experiencing God. Fewer and fewer people are attracted to Christianity in the 'first world' countries because there is so little practice, so little spirituality, in religion.[6]

---

[6] Matthew Fox, *Creation Spirituality* (San Francisco: HarperSanFrancisco, 1991), 75.

## Being spiritual

Partly as a consequence of that, we have become embarrassed by the spiritual, the numinous, the mystical and the supernatural. Some years ago I had a meeting with a Hollywood actress who has emerged as one of the leading spokespersons for the New Age movement. One of her major difficulties with Christianity was, as she put it, that 'the only rationalist-materialists left in the world are all in the churches'. An exaggeration, no doubt – but sufficiently near the mark for us to need to take notice of what she was saying. It is ironic, to say the least, that the church is in serious decline at exactly the same time as our whole culture is experiencing a rising tide of spiritual concern – and that many of today's spiritual search-ers dismiss the church, not because it is irrelevant or old-fashioned, but because in their opinion it is unspiritual. A 'gospel' that has no place for the mystical and the numinous will not be a relevant gospel for the people of today and tomorrow. It would also be somewhat distant from Jesus Christ who – whatever may be in doubt about his sayings and his deeds – is depicted as a healer in every single ancient account of his life, whether written by Christians or others.

## Control

We Western people like to be in control of things – but sometimes the life of the Spirit leads to a certain amount of disorder. Our need for control is partly related to our history (after all, that is how we won our empires), partly to the fact that men have held all the power (and that is how they like to order things), partly also related to the top-heavy models of ministry that the church has adopted. Consistently, wherever the church is growing throughout the world, it is the 'wrong' sort of people who are at the heart of things: women, children, the oppressed, those with nothing – yet who in spiritual terms seem to have everything.

## Belonging

We have lost a vital sense of community. In their origins, ancient trade guilds aimed to provide communities of mutual support and affirmation for their members. That function was largely supplanted with the growth of the welfare state, but that itself has now collapsed in all but name, and the most desperate need of many people in our land is for a place to belong. The breakdown of relationships at all levels is a major source of personal and social disintegration. A friend of mine once wrote a book entitled *Crowded Pews and Lonely People*.[7] She was an American, hence her reference to 'crowded pews': her title would have meant nothing here, where the pews are largely empty. But the reality to which she drew attention is familiar to us all, for the streets of our towns and cities are crowded with lonely people. Our churches too – though they are less crowded than their American counterparts – harbour many lonely people. All around us, people are asking big questions: Who am I? Where do I fit in? How can I make the best use of this life God has given me? All too often, they find neither understanding nor acceptance among Christians. Yet the Jesus presented to us in the New Testament consistently identified the reality of loving community as one of the key aspects of Christian discipleship – and in the early centuries even those who opposed the church often commended Christians for their love of one another. Those churches that are growing in the West (and there are some) are those that have seen the need to be open, inclusive and welcoming, and have worked hard at creating and nurturing effective community.

## Suffering

Finally, suffering plays a major part in the life of the world church today. In David Barrett's annual update of the statistics of world Christianity, he includes a column for Christian martyrs. How many Christians do you think died for their faith in 1996? Twenty or thirty? A hundred, maybe? The answer is a staggering 159,000.[8] Following Jesus is not a soft option. That ought not to surprise us.

---

[7] Marion Leach Jacobsen, *Crowded Pews and Lonely People* (Wheaton, IL: Tyndale House Publishers, 1976).

[8] The statistics for 1999, the latest available, show the current annual figure as 164,000. Cf. David M. Barrett and Todd M. Johnson, 'Annual Statistical Table on Global Mission: 1999', in *International Bulletin of Missionary Research* 23/1 (January 1999), 24–25.

Do you think Jesus himself was a successful man? If he were here today, who would sponsor his ministry? Jesus offers a hard challenge: 'Take up your cross and follow me' (Mark 8:34). Yet it is a challenge with a promise. For those who will follow, Jesus also offers a dynamic vision with the potential to transform the whole of life. Our personal thinking, our feelings, our relationships, emotions – these are all included. Moreover, this vision goes beyond the needs of individuals, and ultimately offers the possibility of transformation for the entire cosmos, embraced by a spirituality that is vibrant and alive. It is a vision in which the wounded and broken-hearted are lifted up, in which those who are nobodies can become somebody, where new commitments can create community among the most unlikely of folk, as ordinary people empowered by God's Spirit find themselves able to do extraordinary things. To those who share this vision, and who would like to see the world this way, Jesus' call is as vital and relevant as ever it was: Come and take up your cross, and follow me. Bring the baggage of your own life, whatever it might be – for that is part of the cross we bear – and join him on a journey toward personal and cultural transformation and fulfilment. It is not an easy pathway, it might even be painful, and we can only decide for ourselves whether it is worth the cost.

## The Promise of New Life

During the late fifteenth and early sixteenth centuries, Italy was home to many skilled artists, including the uniquely gifted Michelangelo. One day he was presented with a half-made statue that some lesser sculptor had begun to work. The marble had a certain attractiveness, but it was not easy to carve. The grain seemed to be going in all the wrong directions, and the stone was constantly splitting in unpredictable ways whenever the chisel was applied to it. It would not be easy even for someone of Michelangelo's prowess to make much of it. As he worked patiently, passers-by would stop and stare. Someone asked him, 'Michelangelo, why are you wasting your time with such unpromising material?' His answer: 'I am releasing the angel imprisoned in this block of stone.' Craftspeople of all kinds know the satisfaction in doing that – of taking rough and unpromising materials, and transforming them into something beautiful. Following Jesus Christ may be hard and challenging, but that is the promise behind the challenge. For all over the world today, people whose lives are shattered and broken, whose relationships lie in pieces, whose best hopes have ended in tragedy, and whose life conflicts seem to have no resolution – they are hearing Jesus' call to take up the cross and to follow him. And as the Spirit of God gets to work, the most remarkable angels are being released from the most unlikely of materials. Do you have the courage to come and join them?